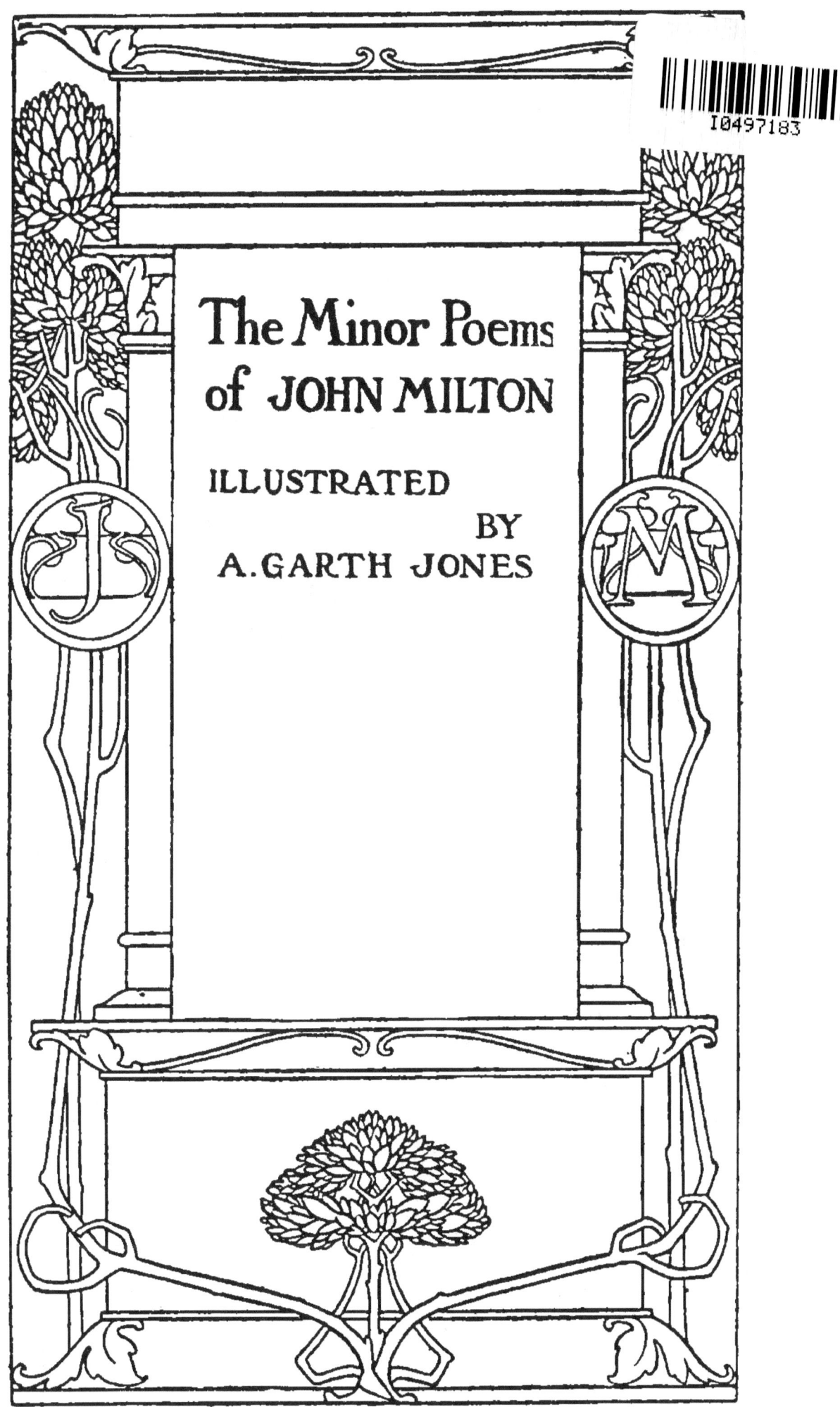

The Minor Poems of JOHN MILTON

ILLUSTRATED BY A. GARTH JONES

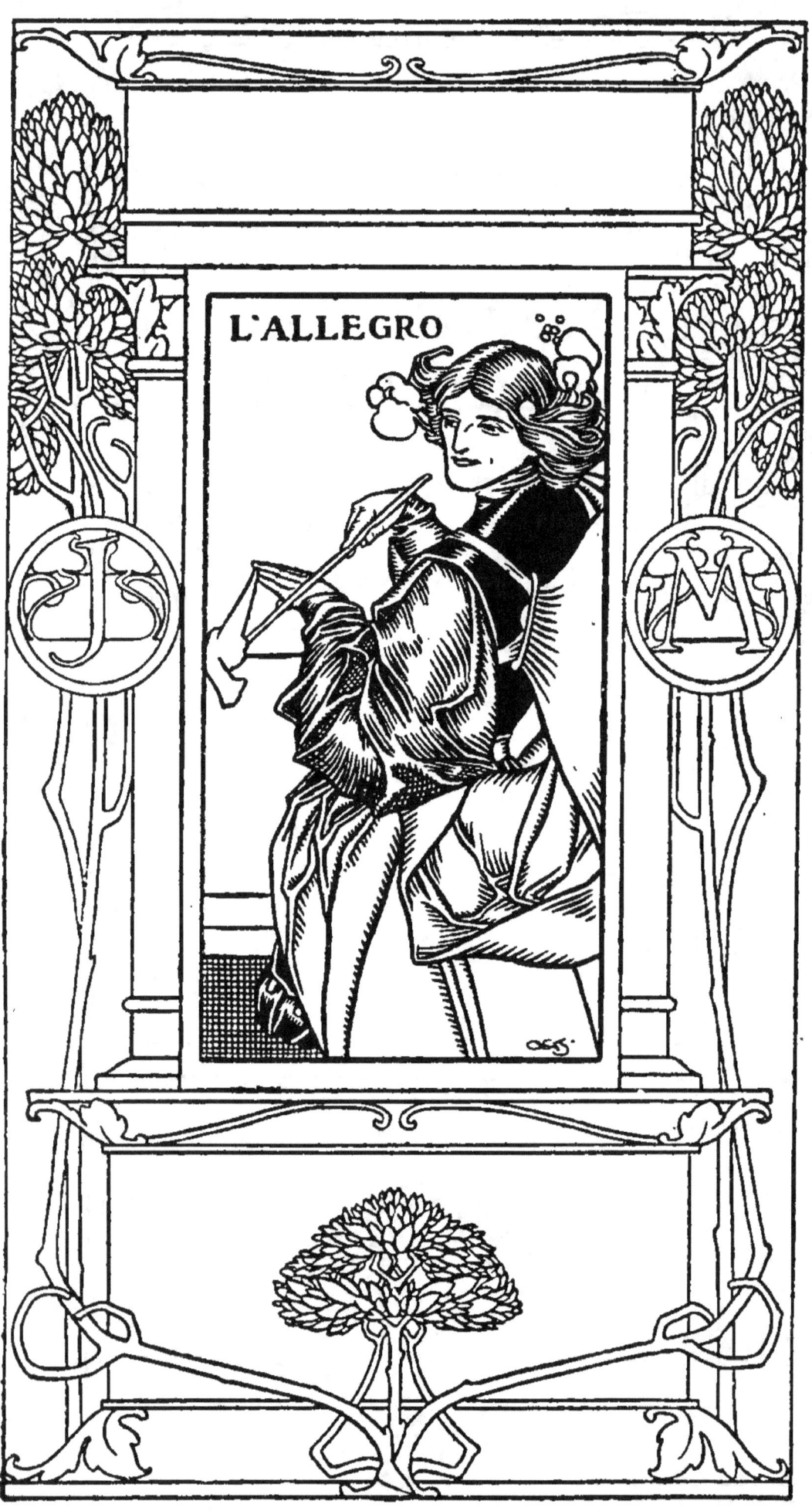

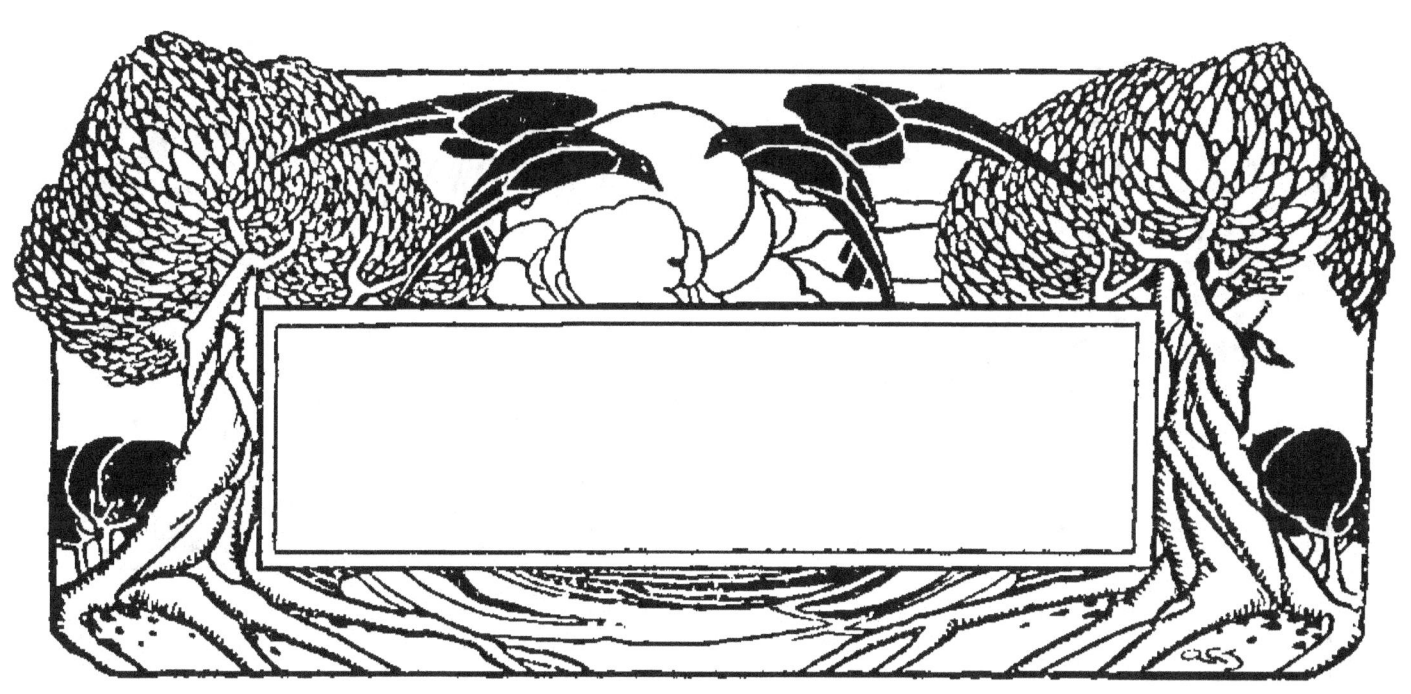

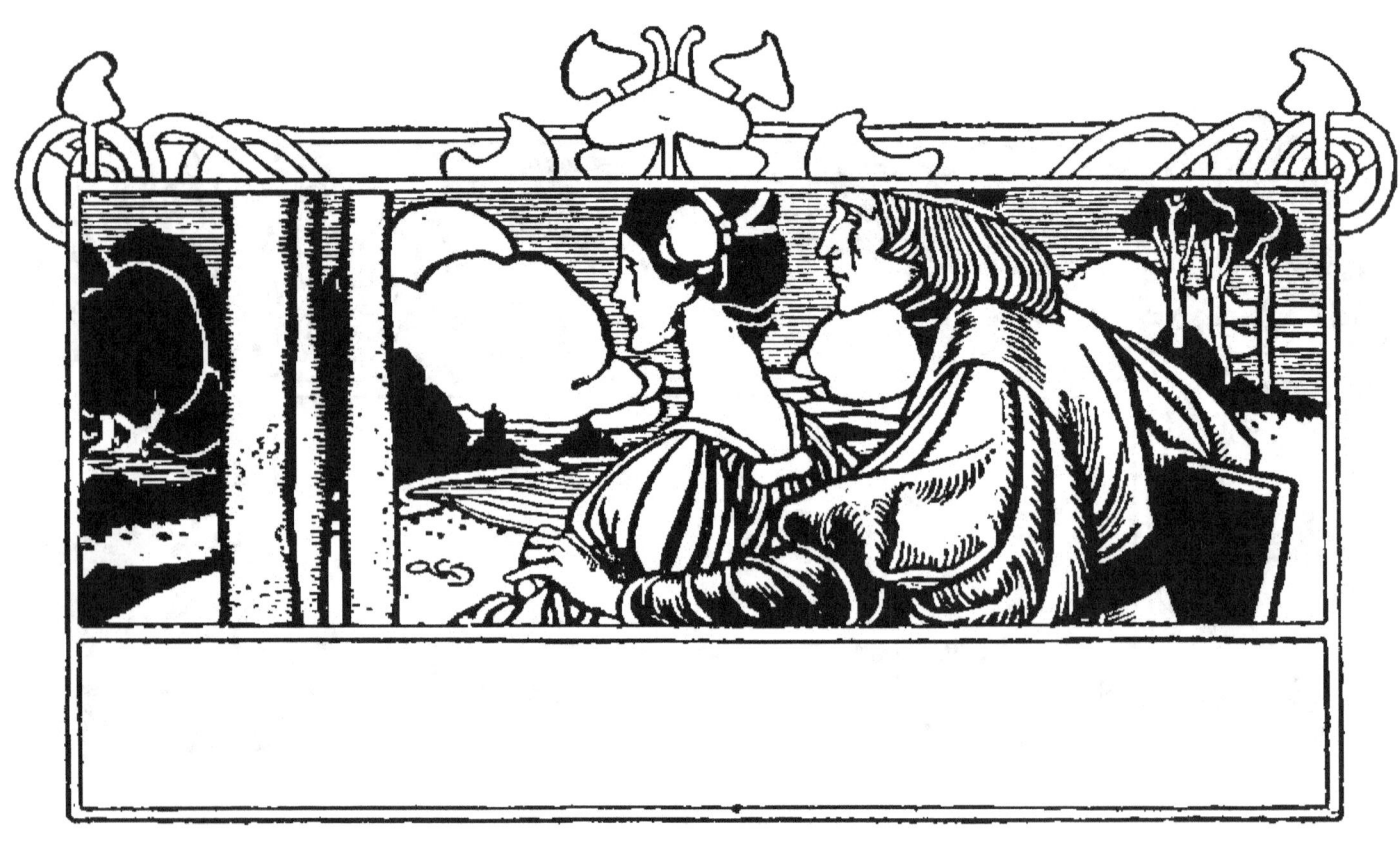

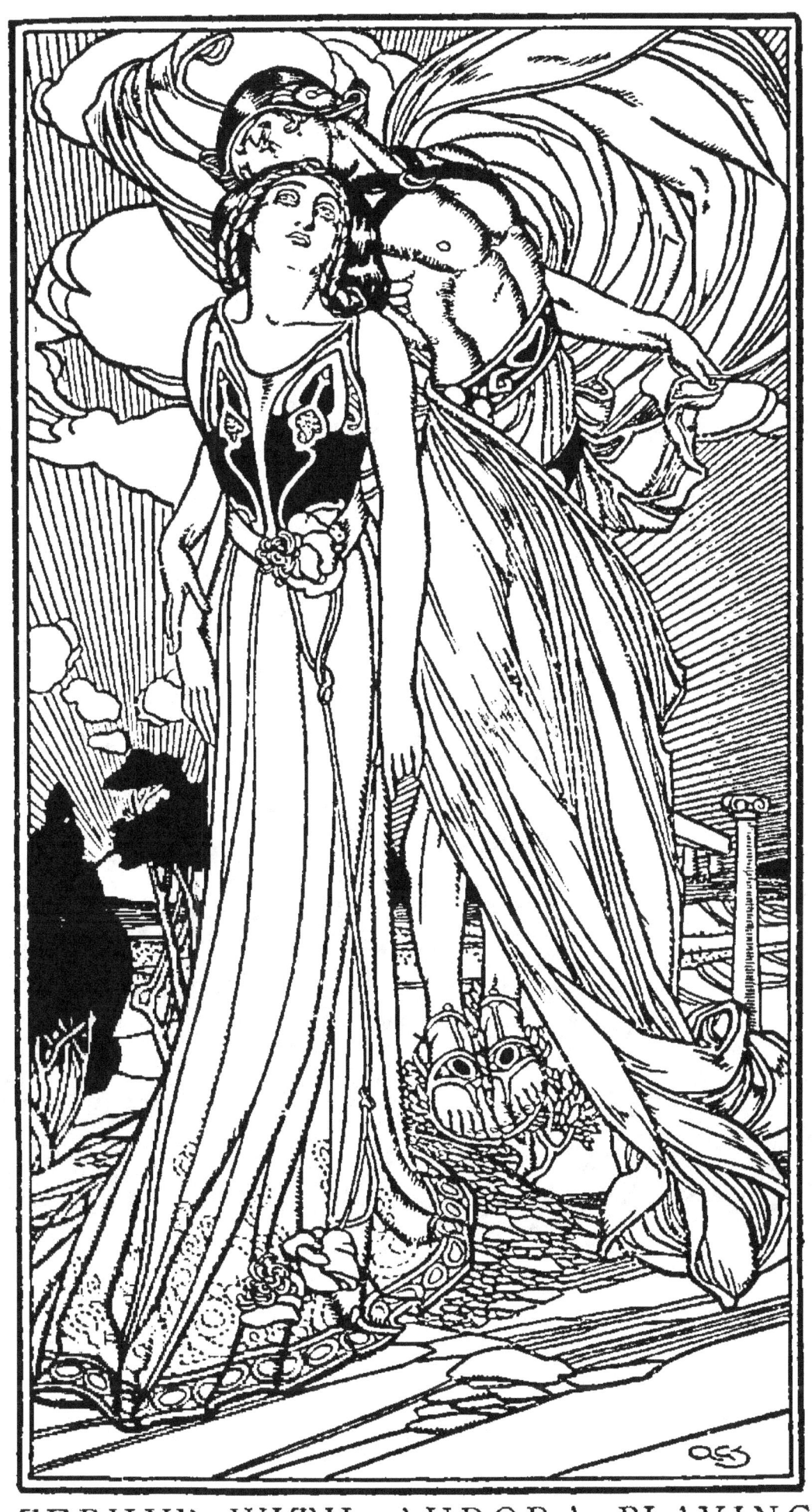

ZEPHYR WITH AURORA PLAYING
AS HE MET HER ONCE A-MAYING

POEMS BY JOHN MILTON

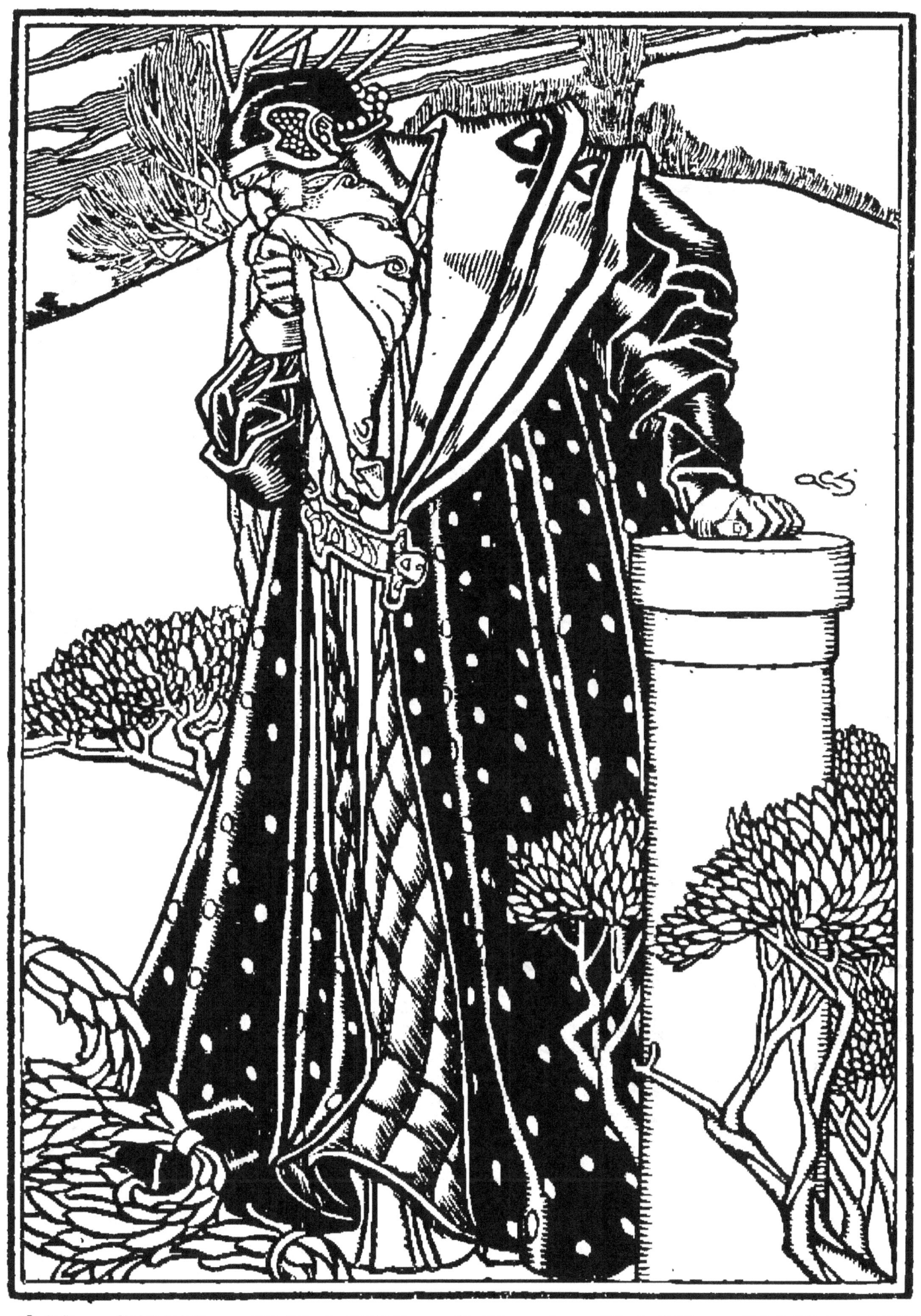

ON THE DEATH OF A FAIR INFANT

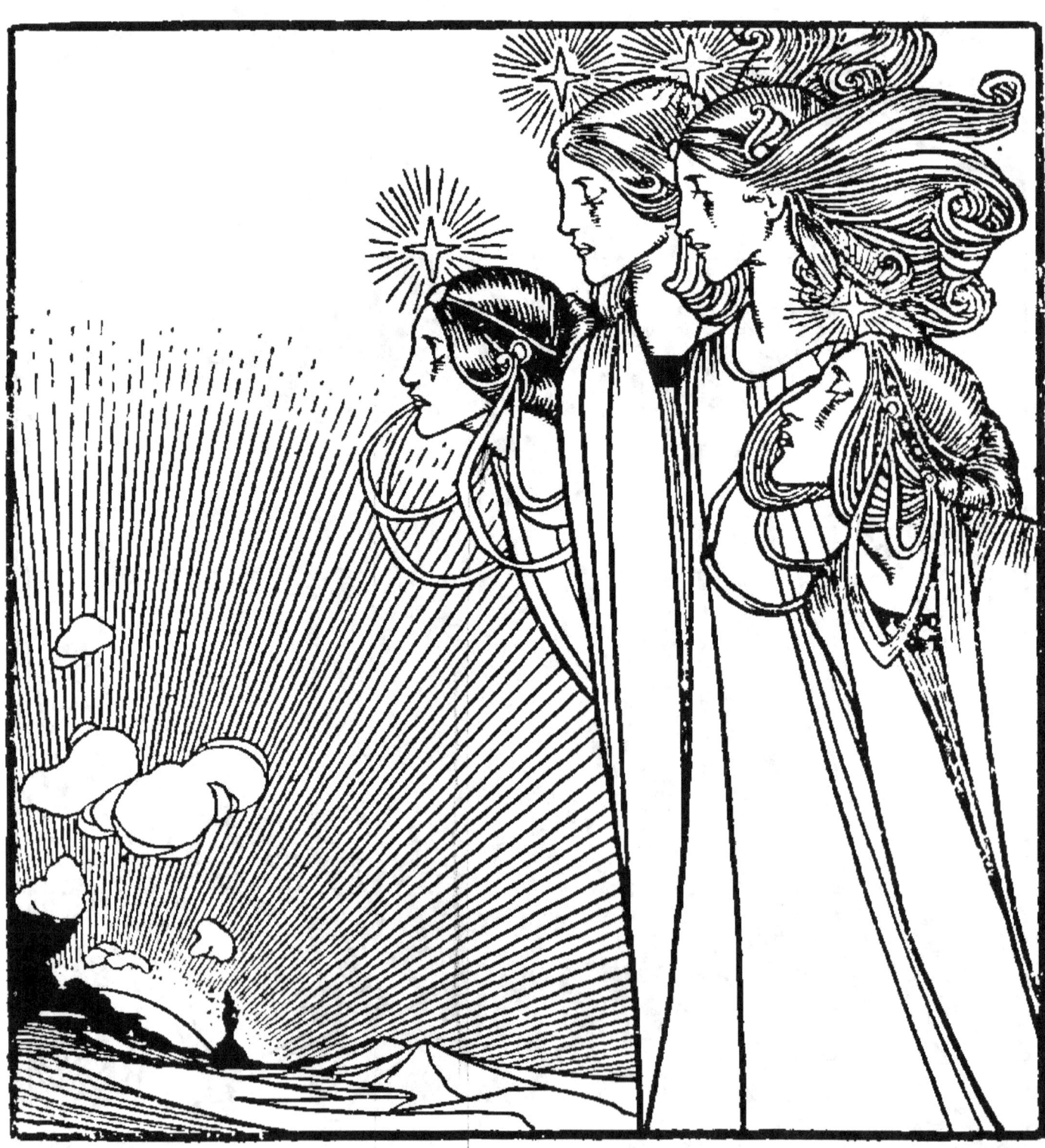

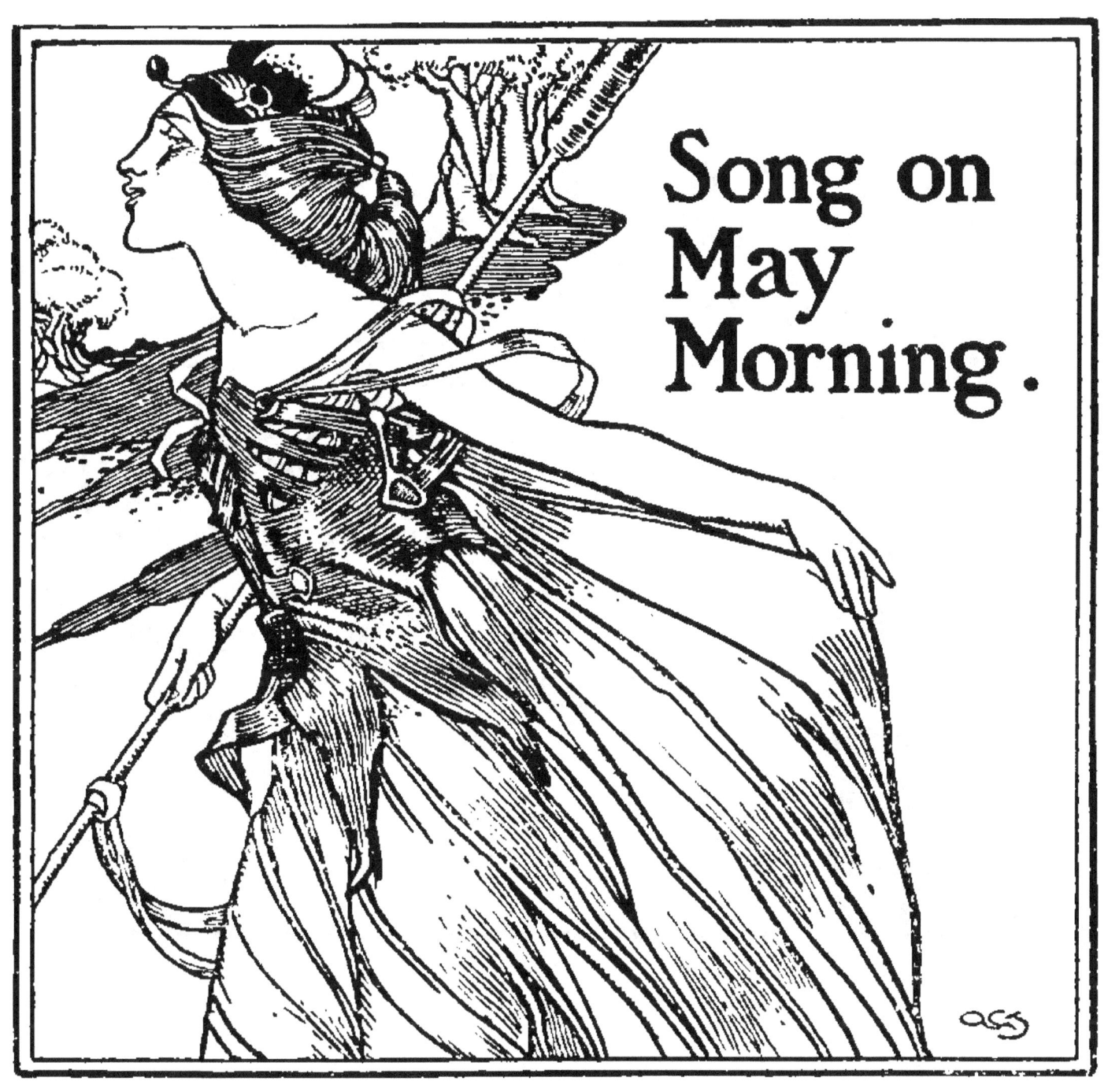

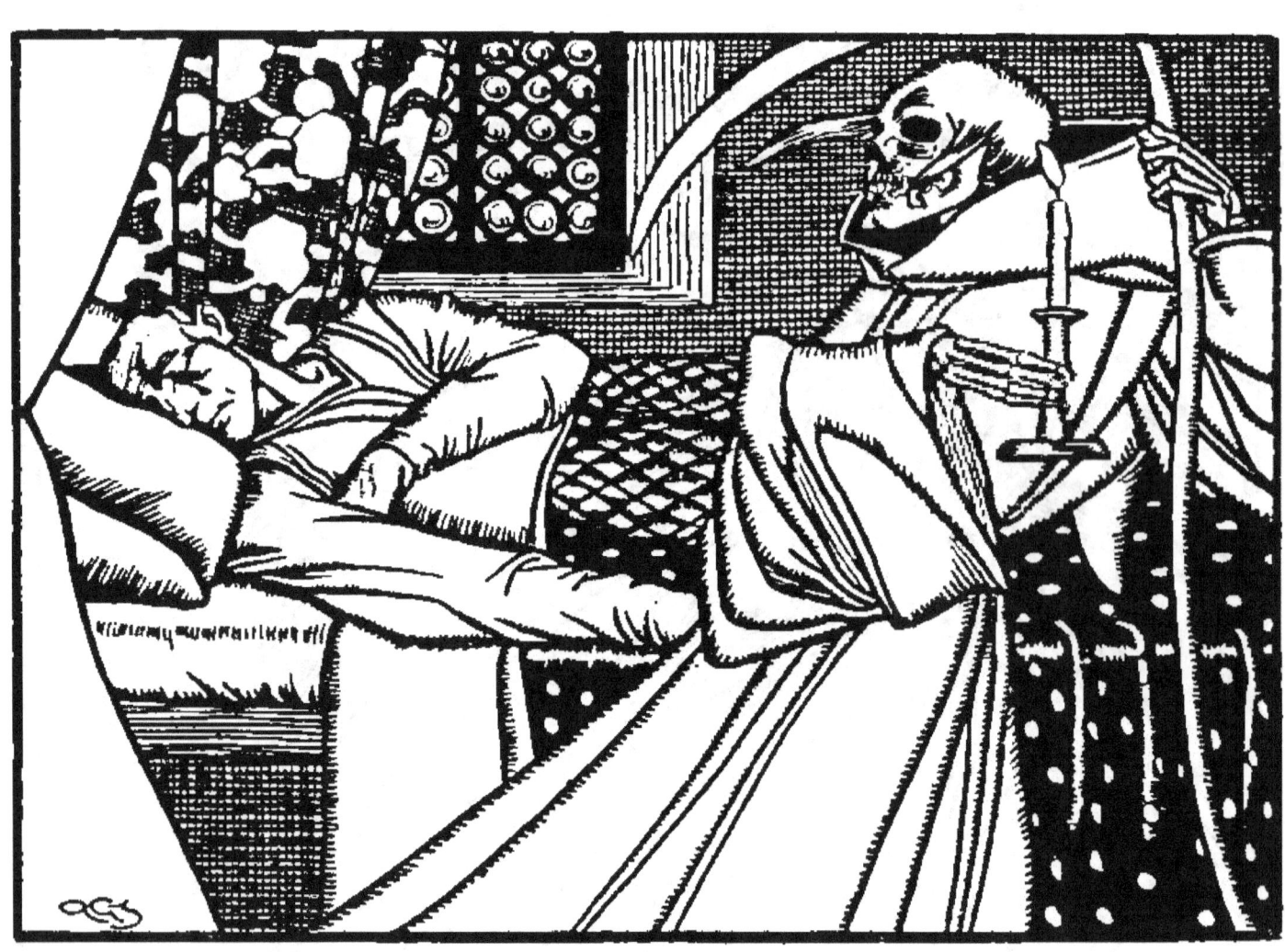

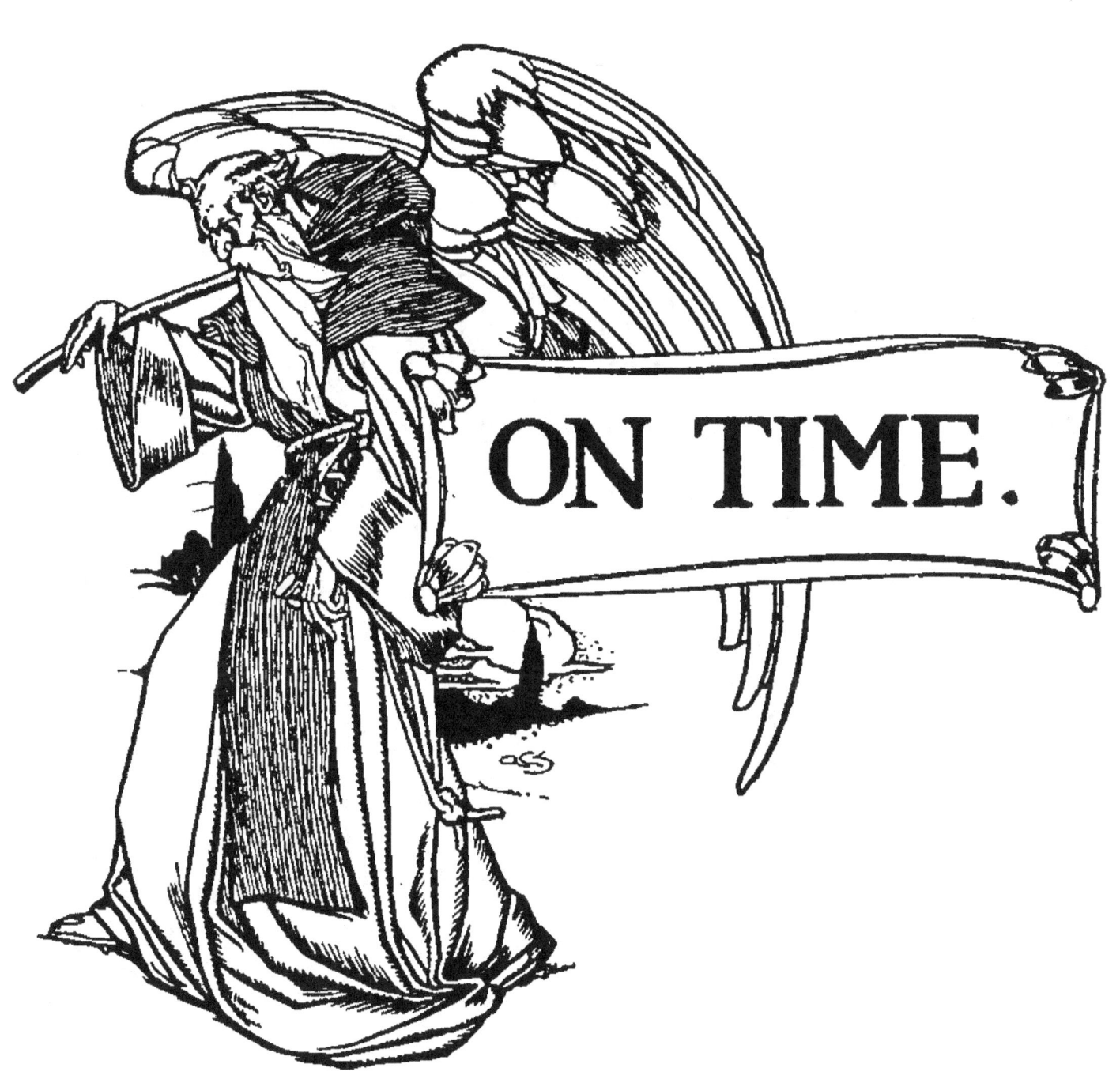

At a Solemn Music.

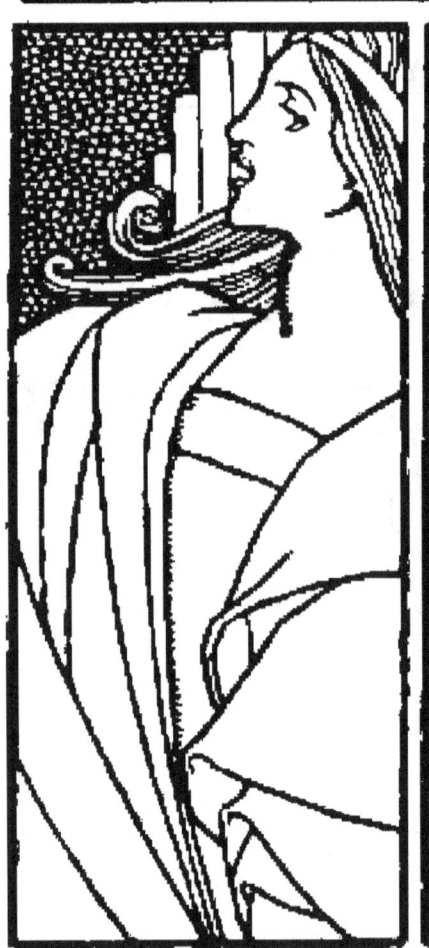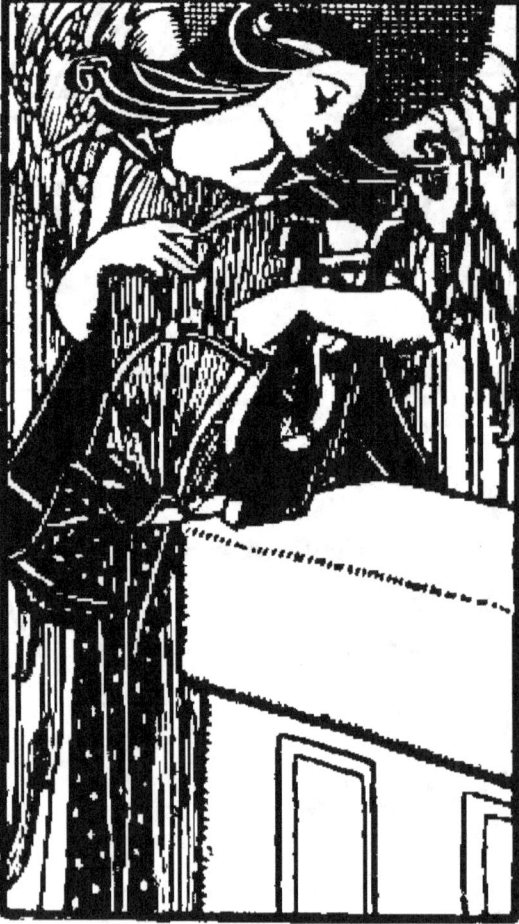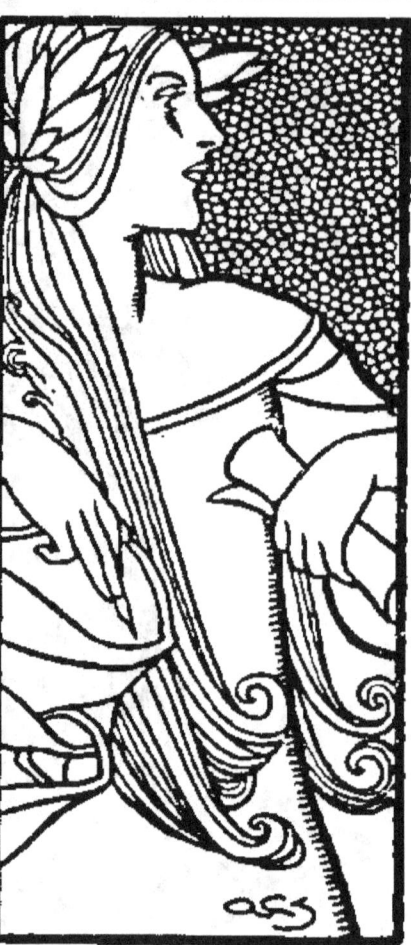

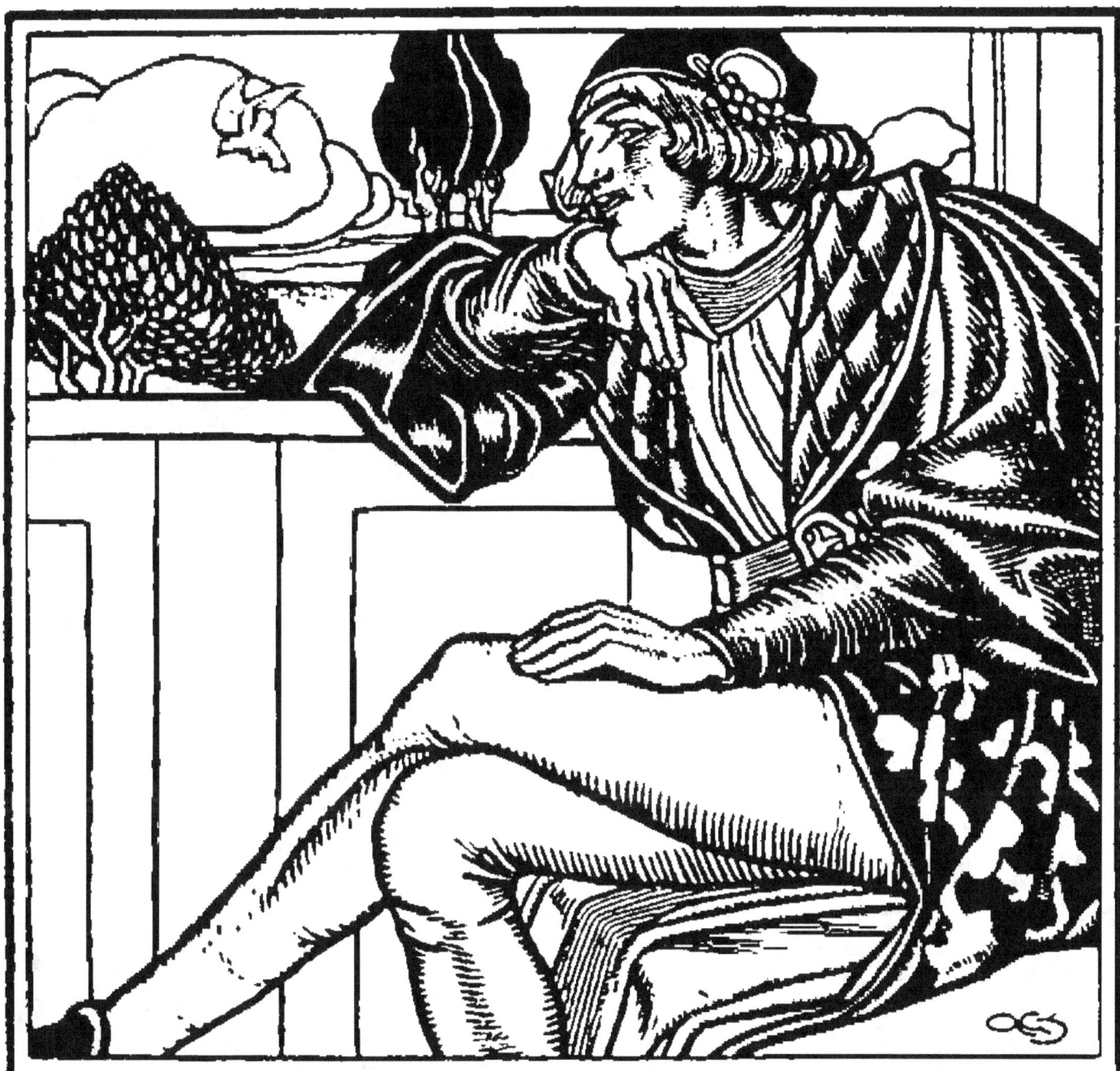

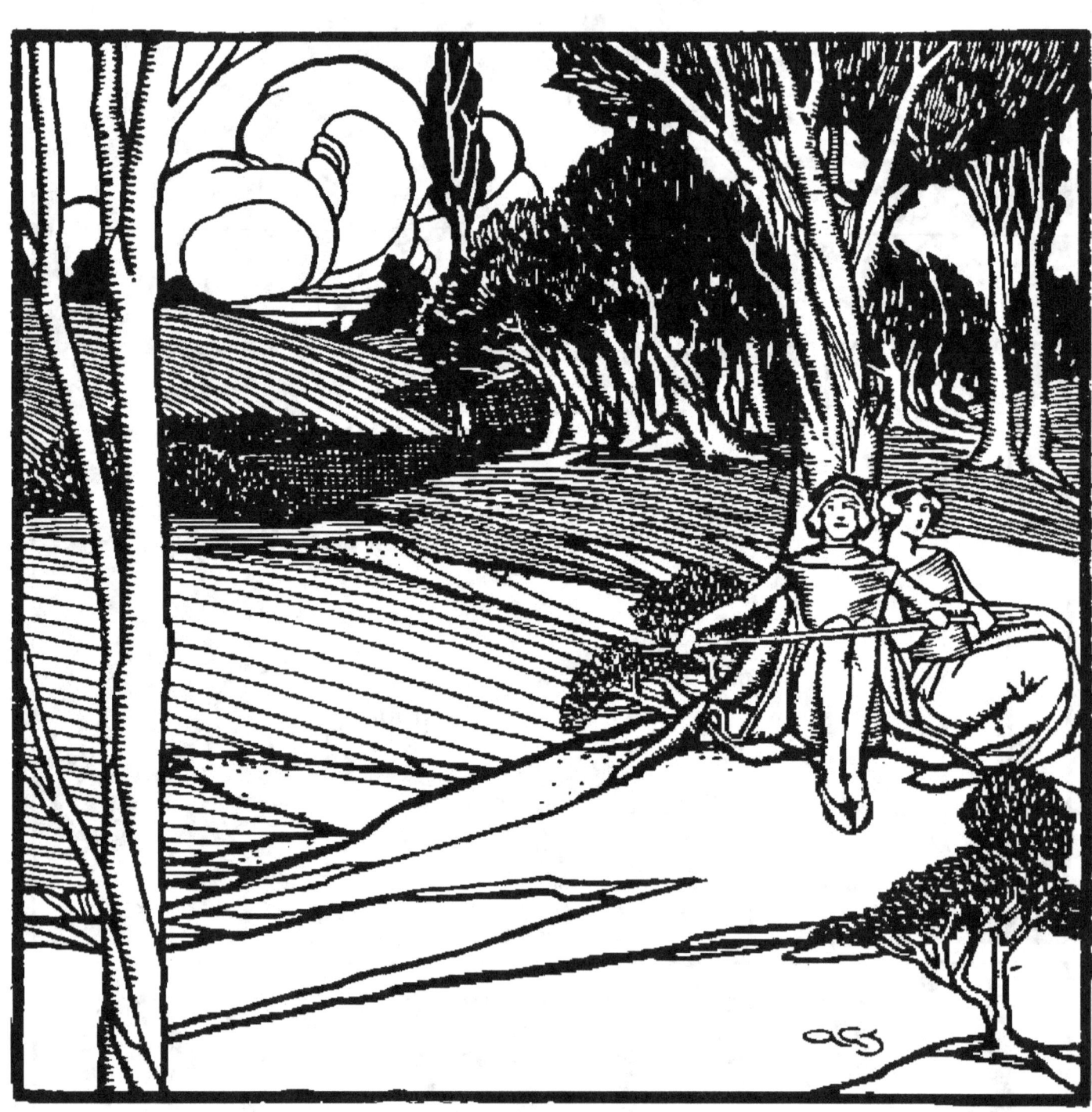

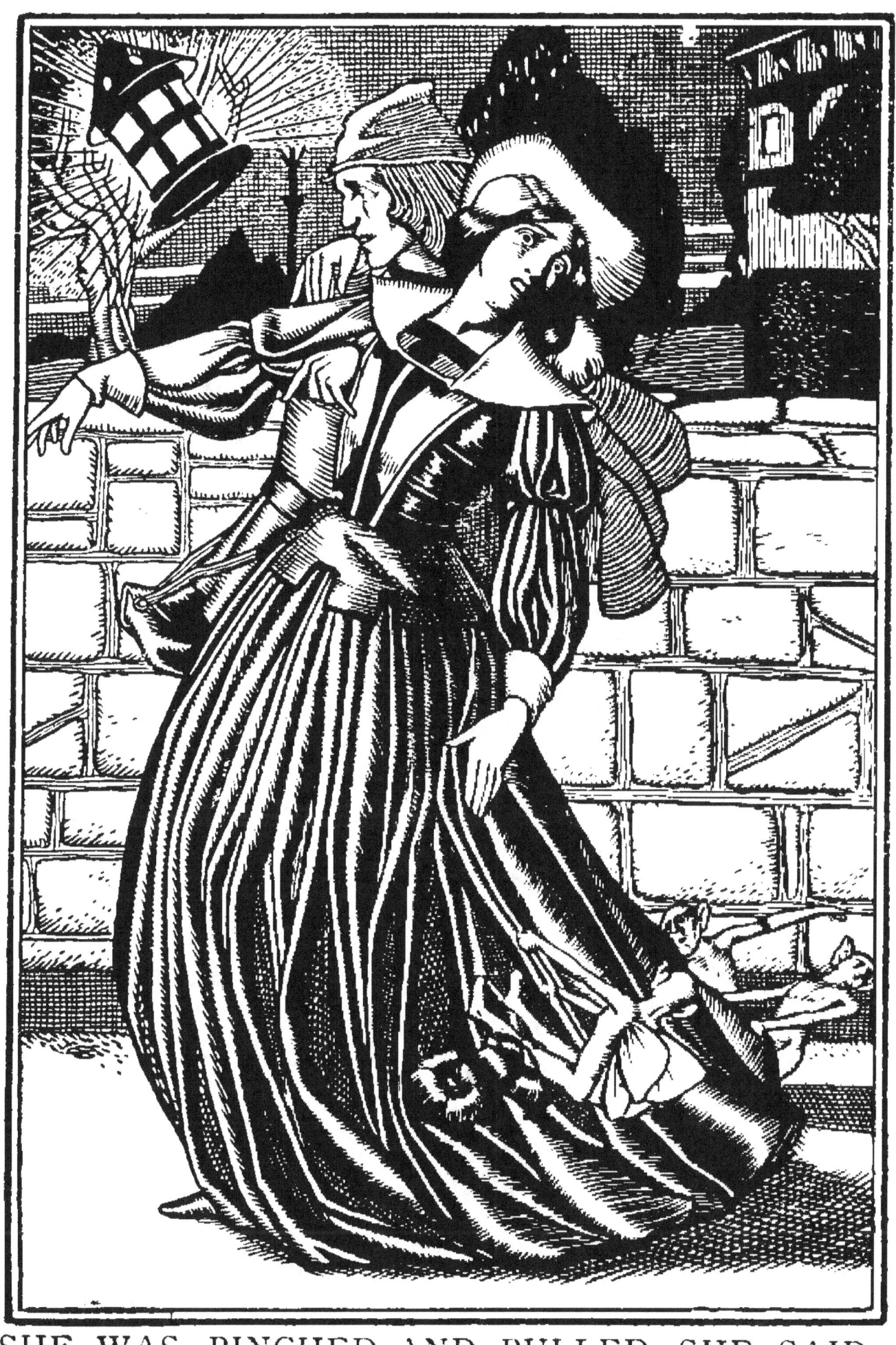

SHE WAS PINCHED AND PULLED, SHE SAID;
AND HE, BY FRIAR'S LANTERN LED

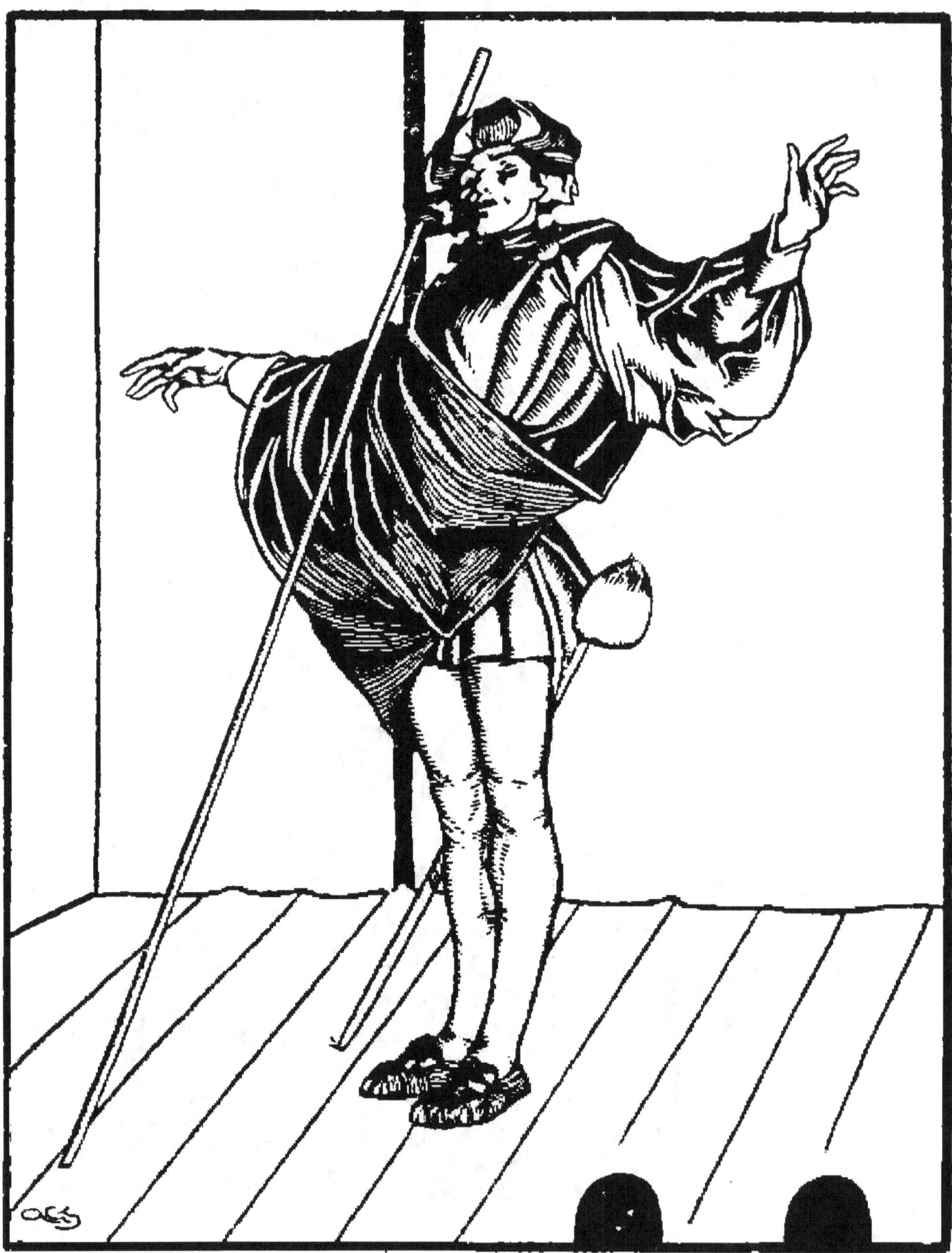

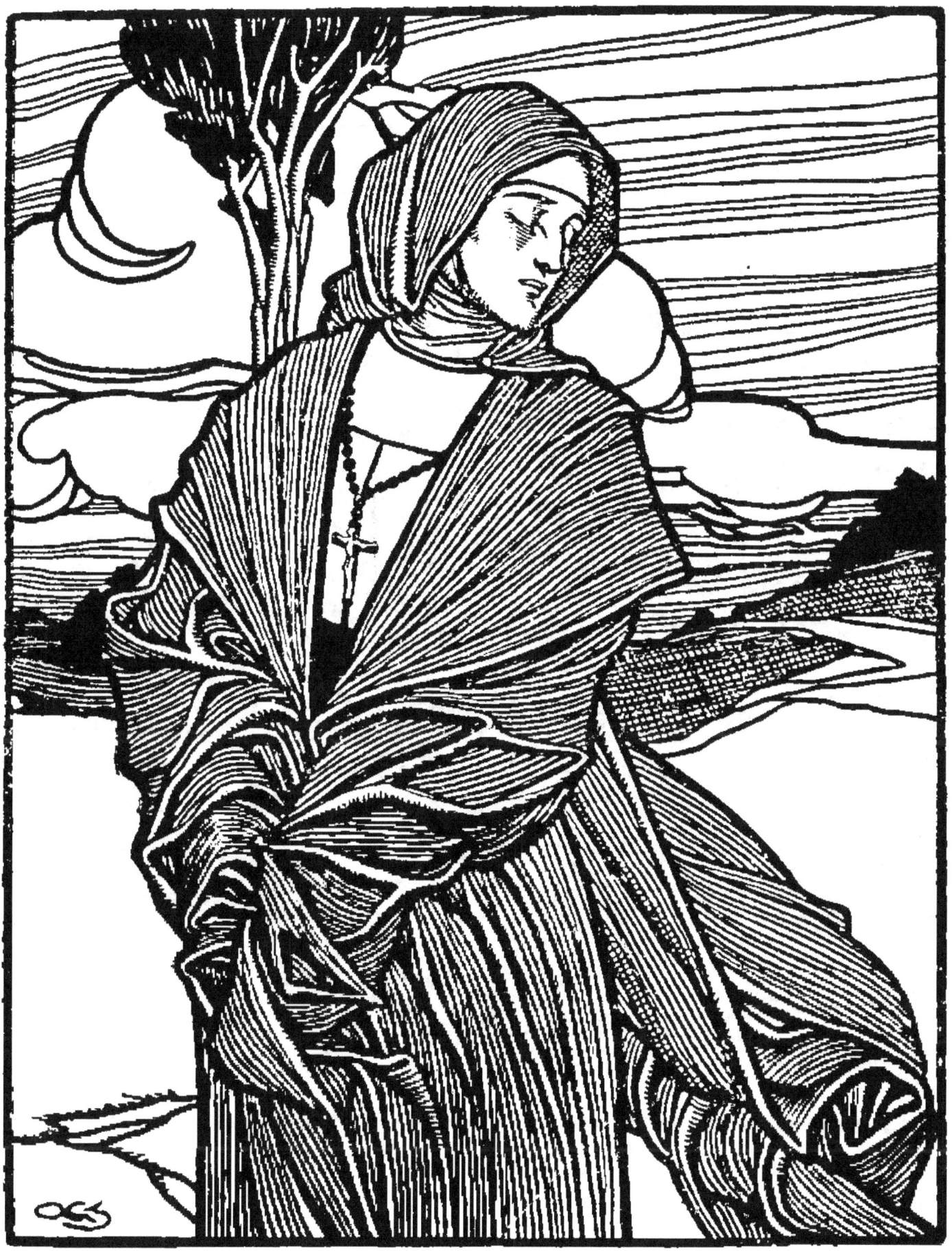

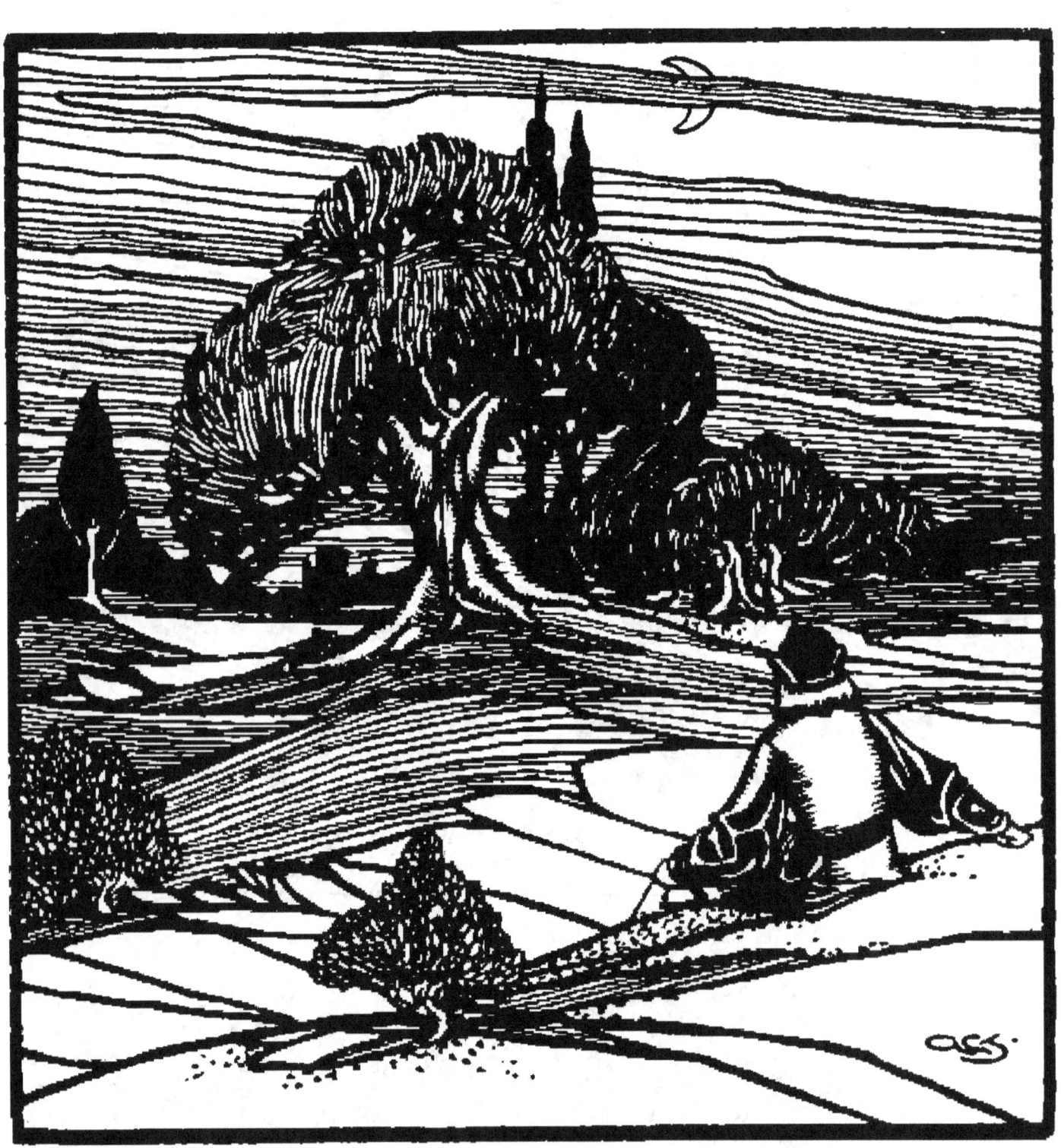

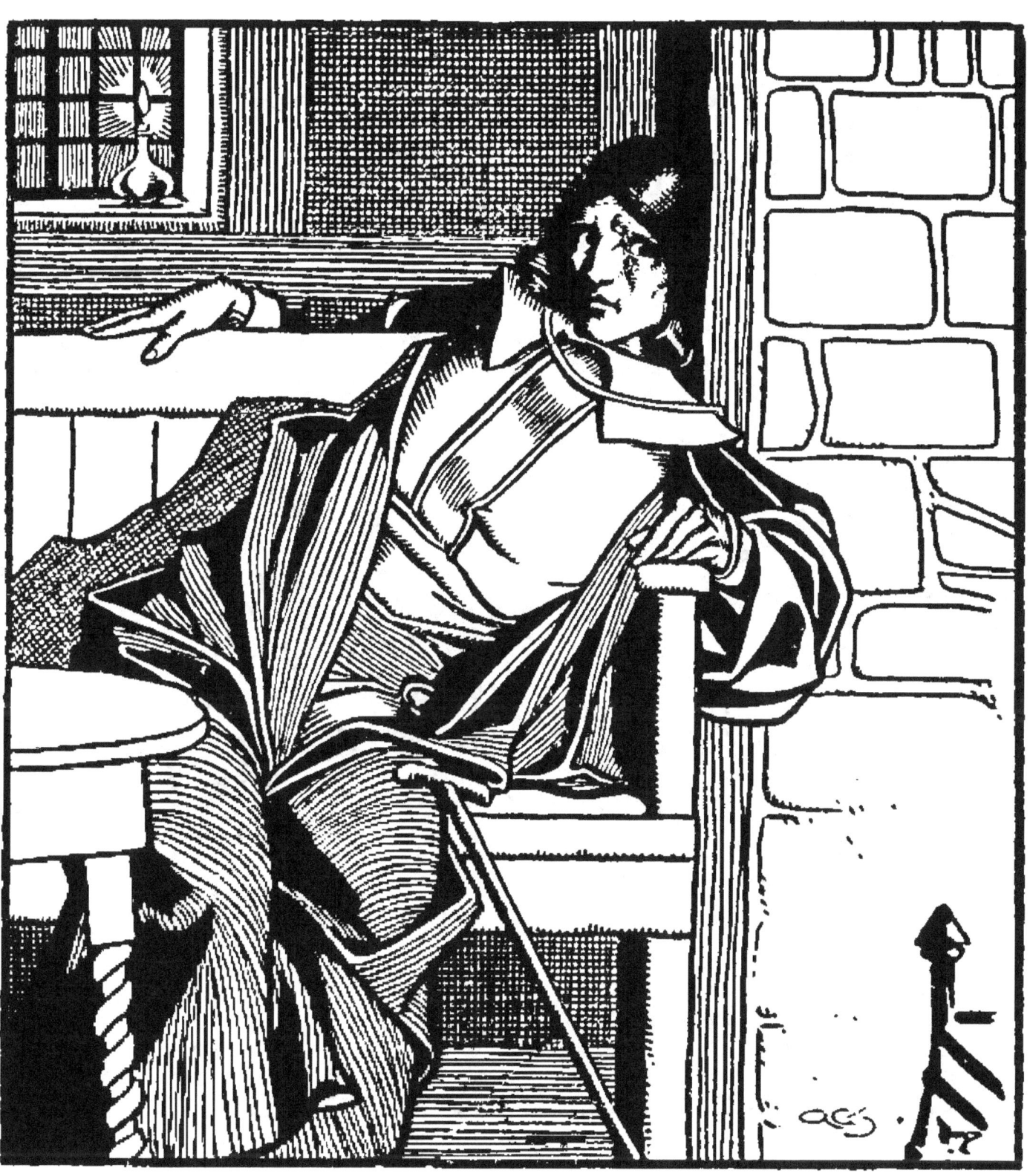

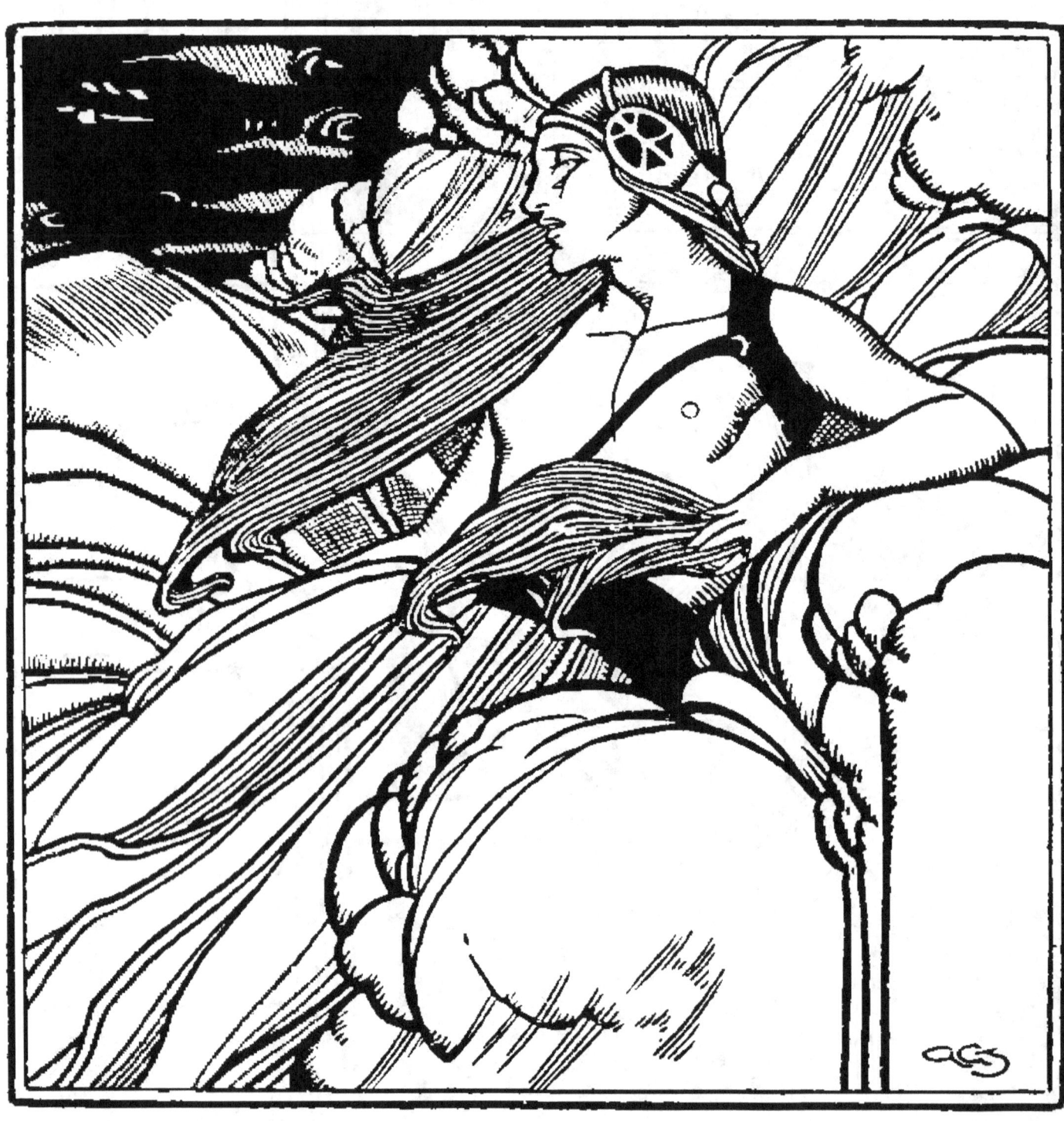

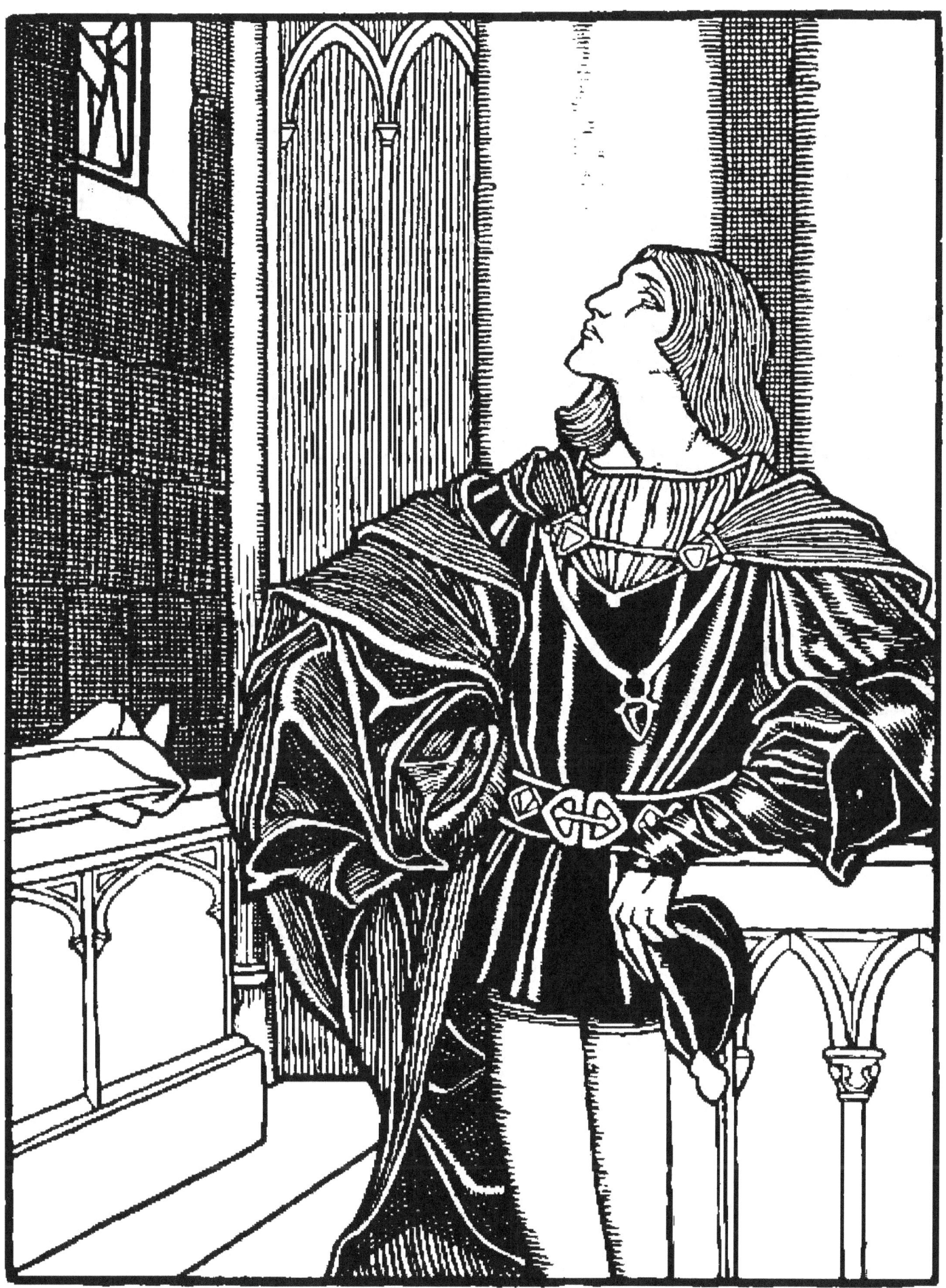

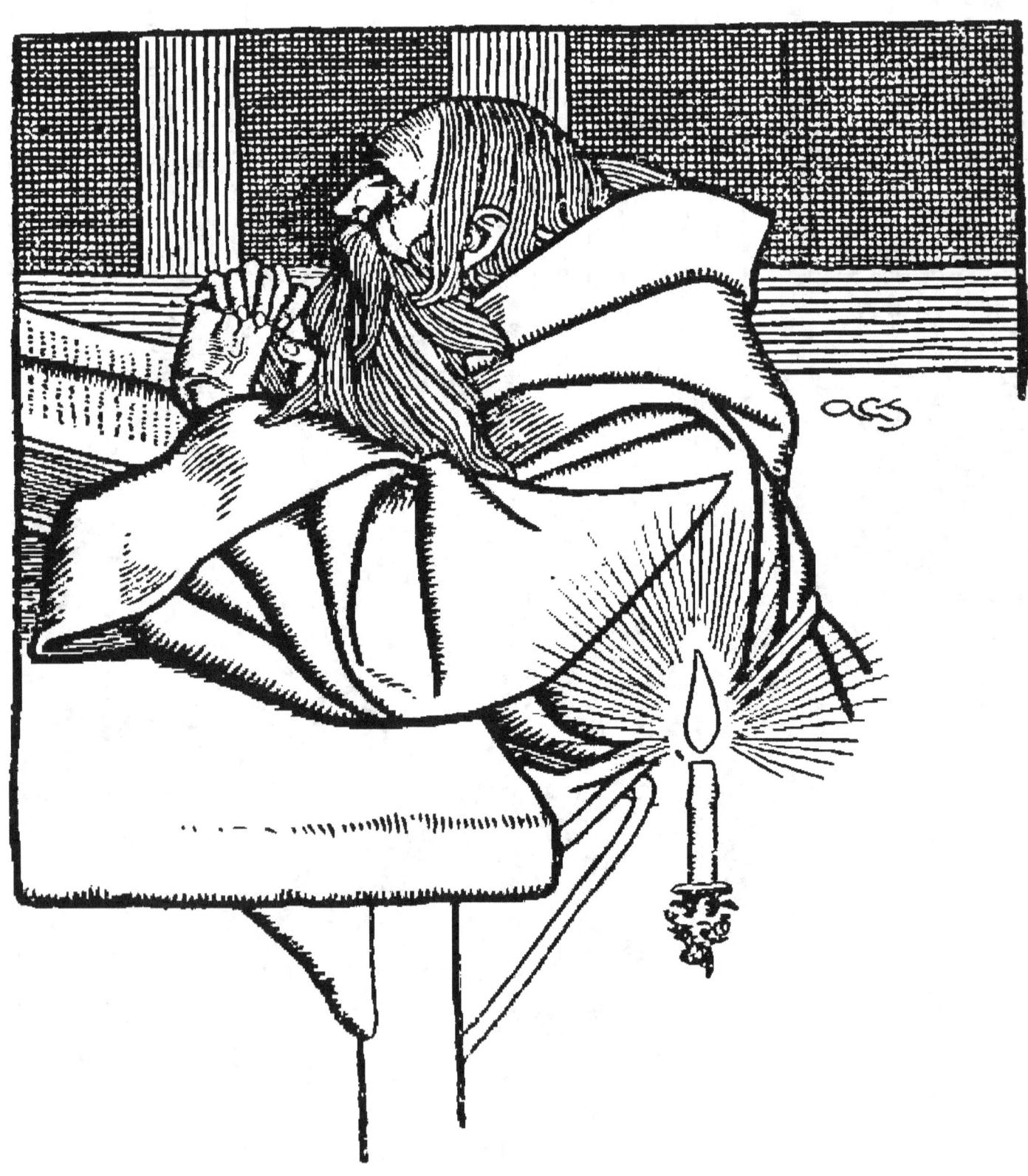

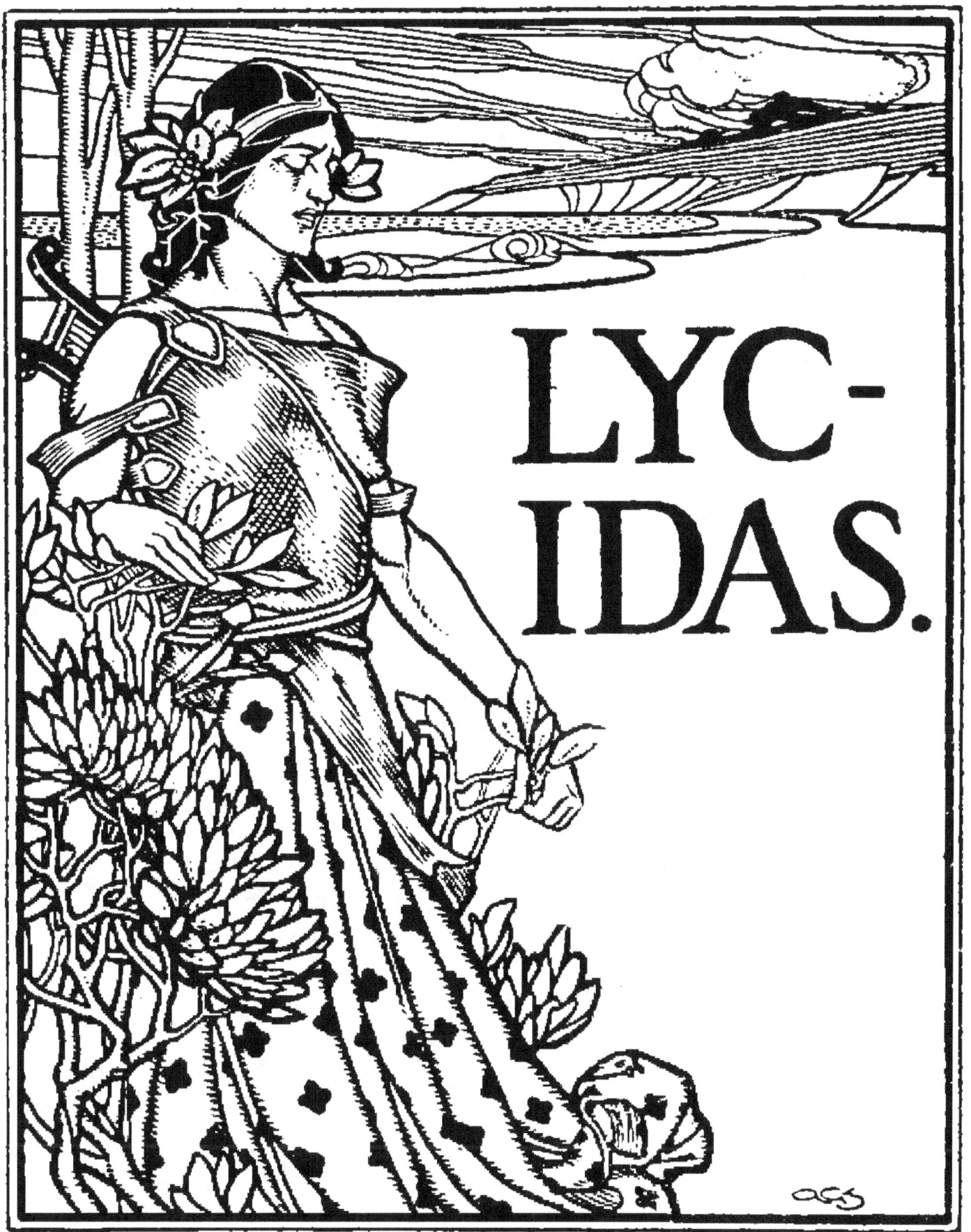

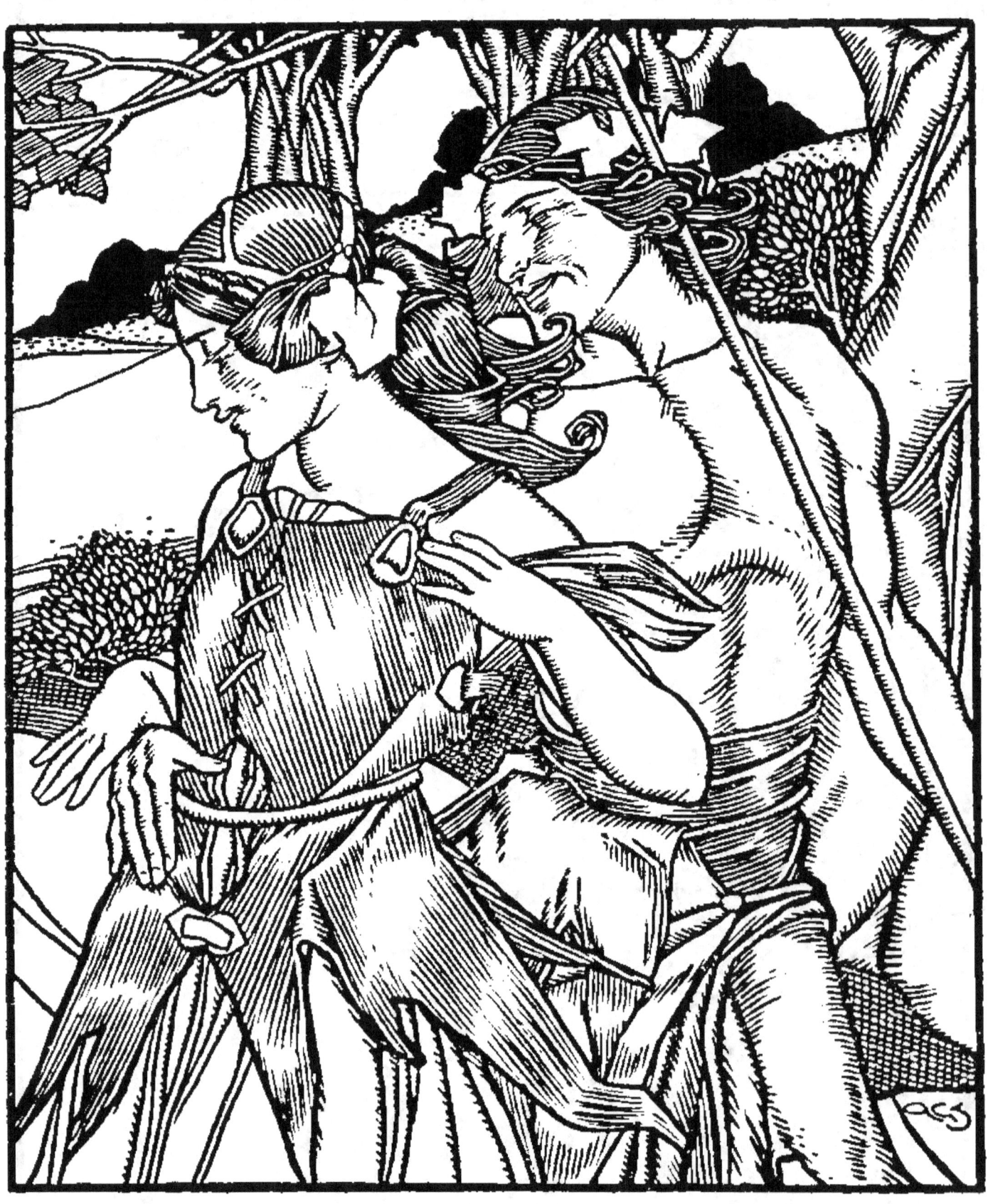

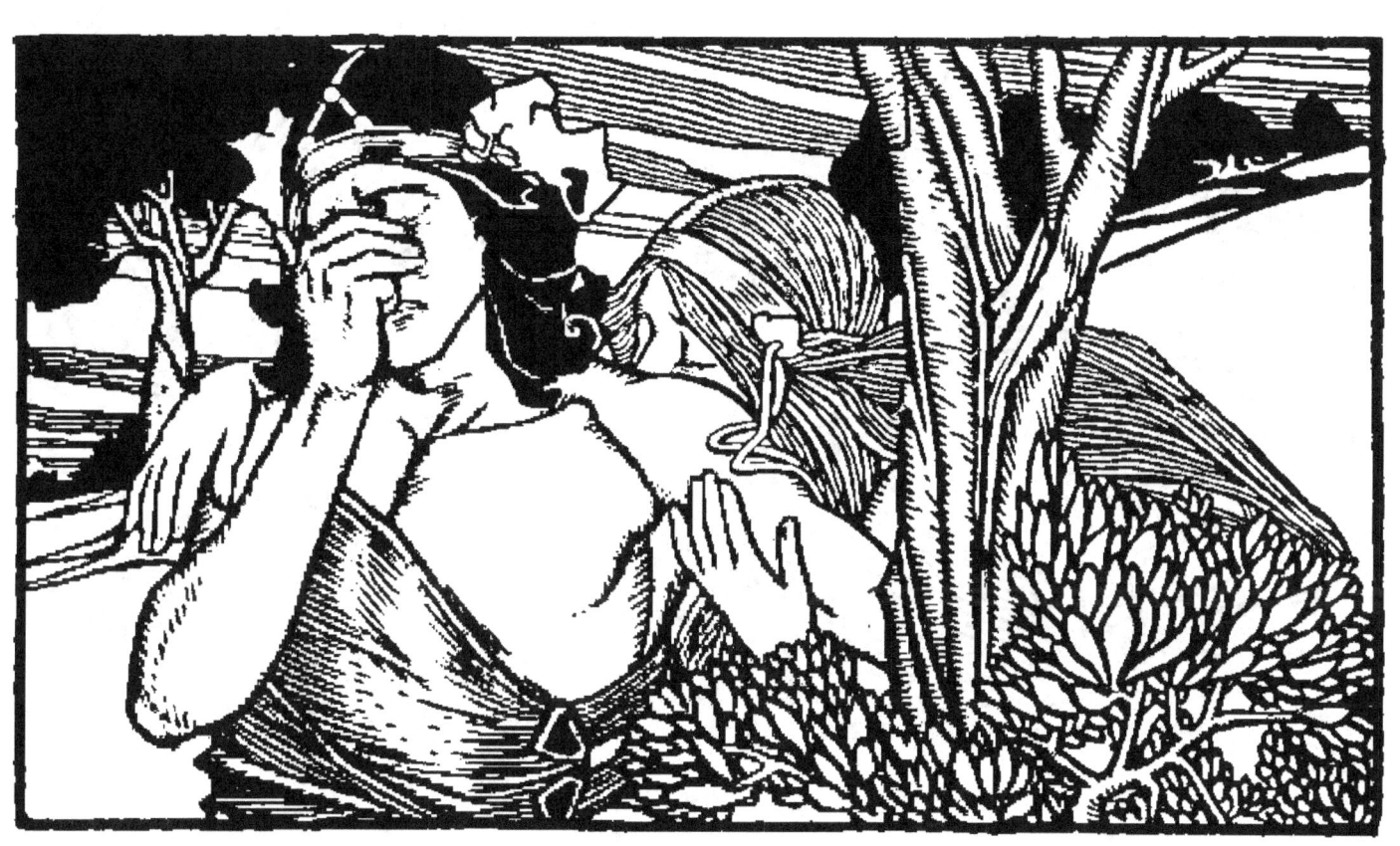

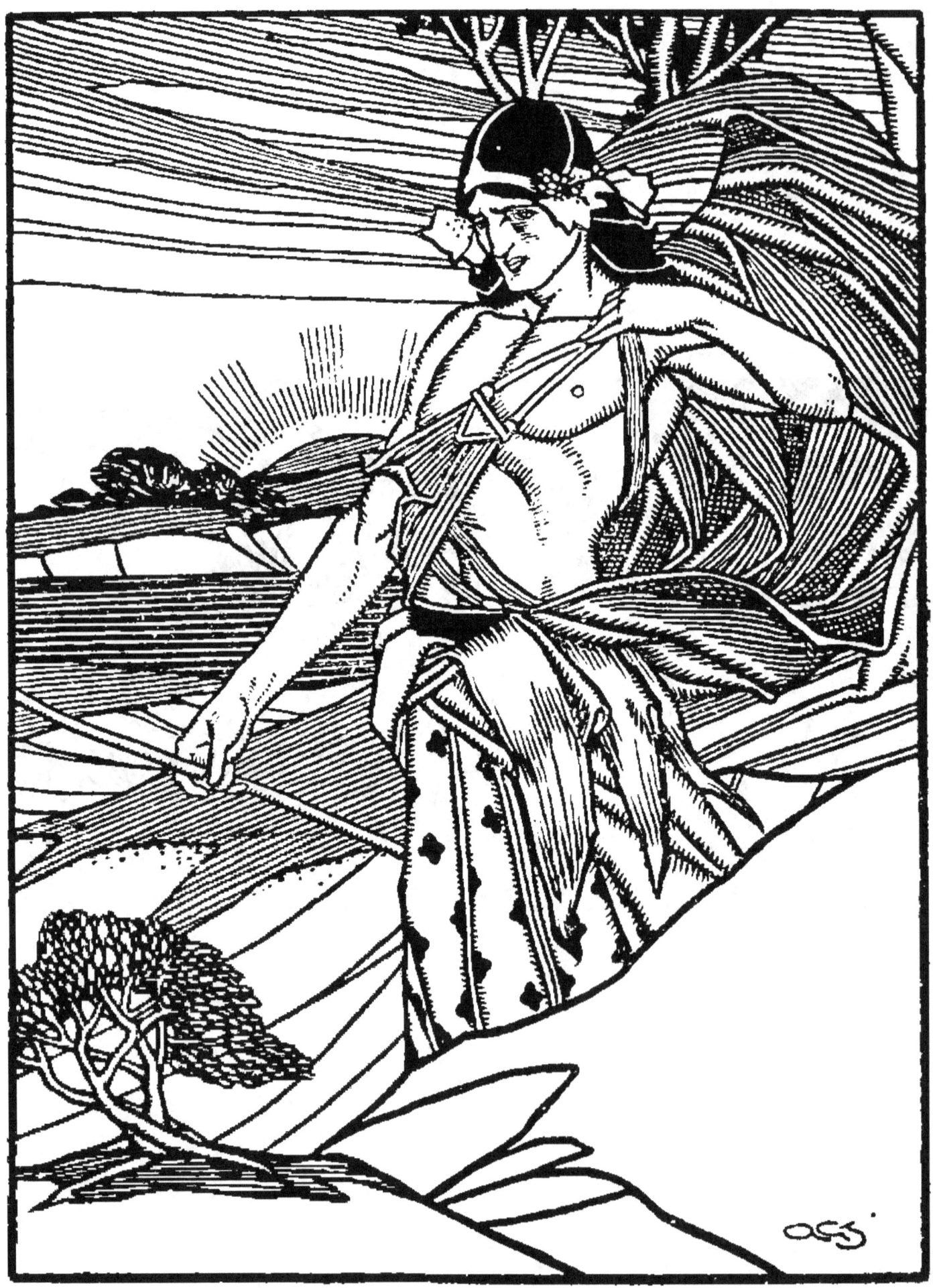

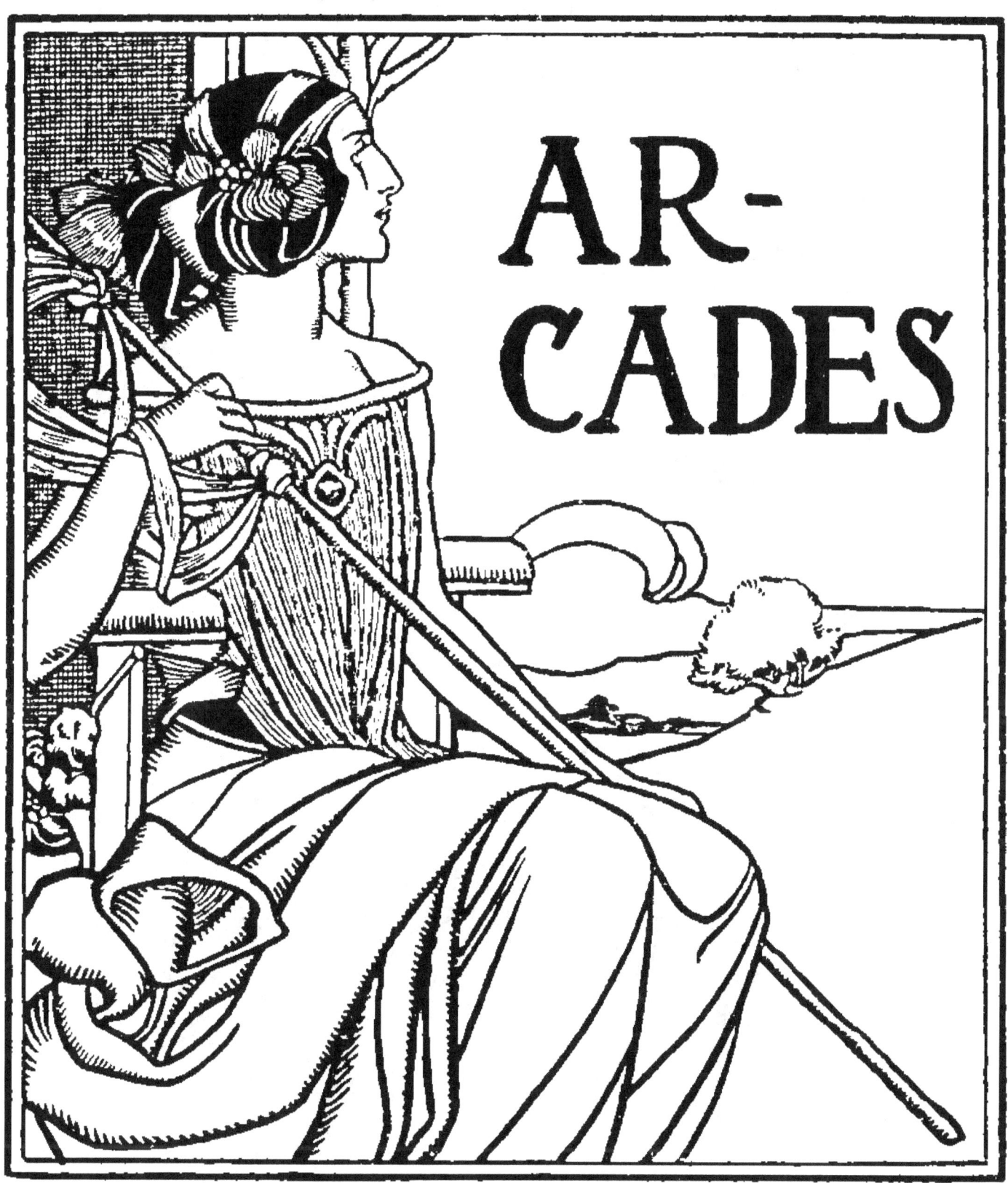

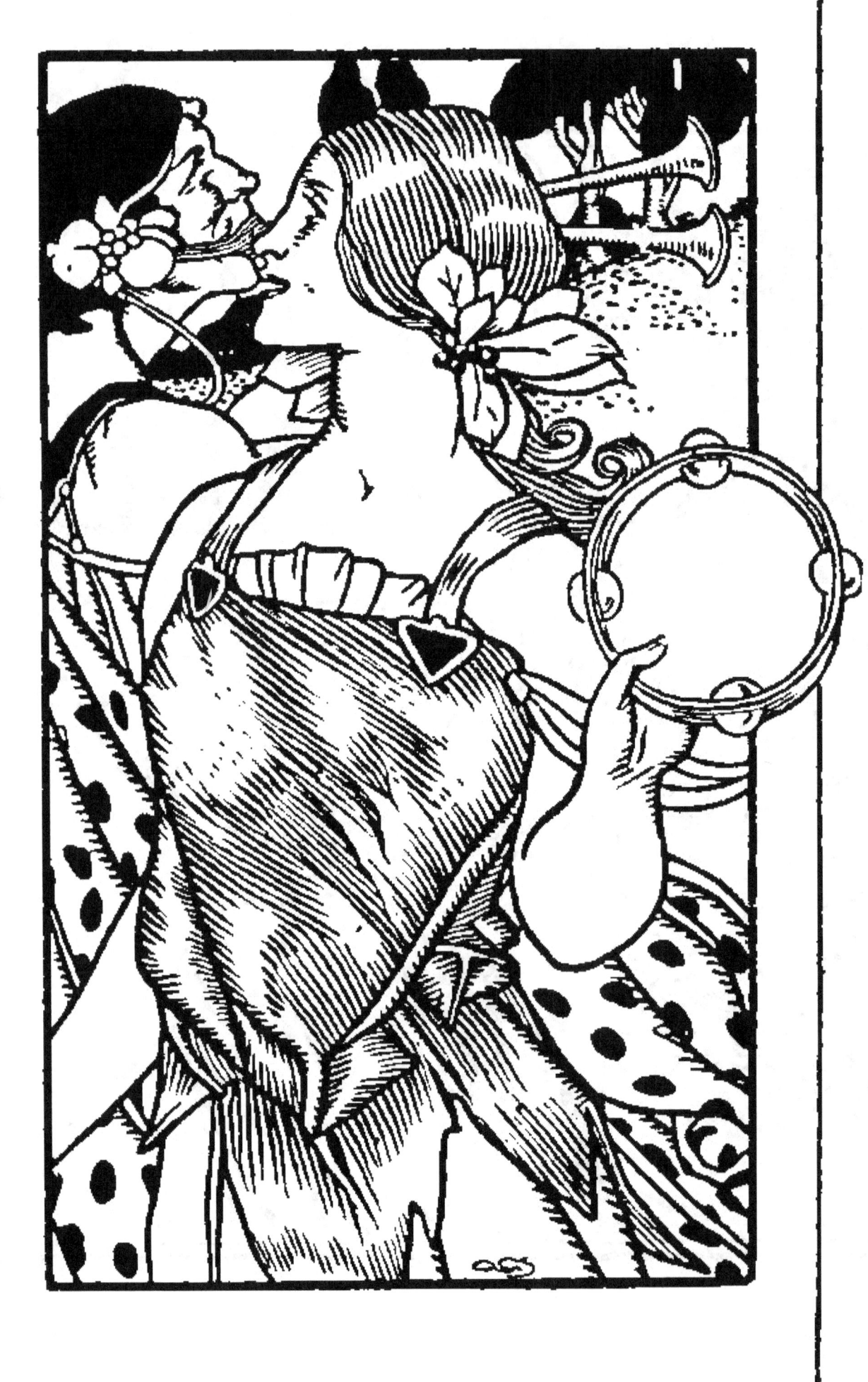

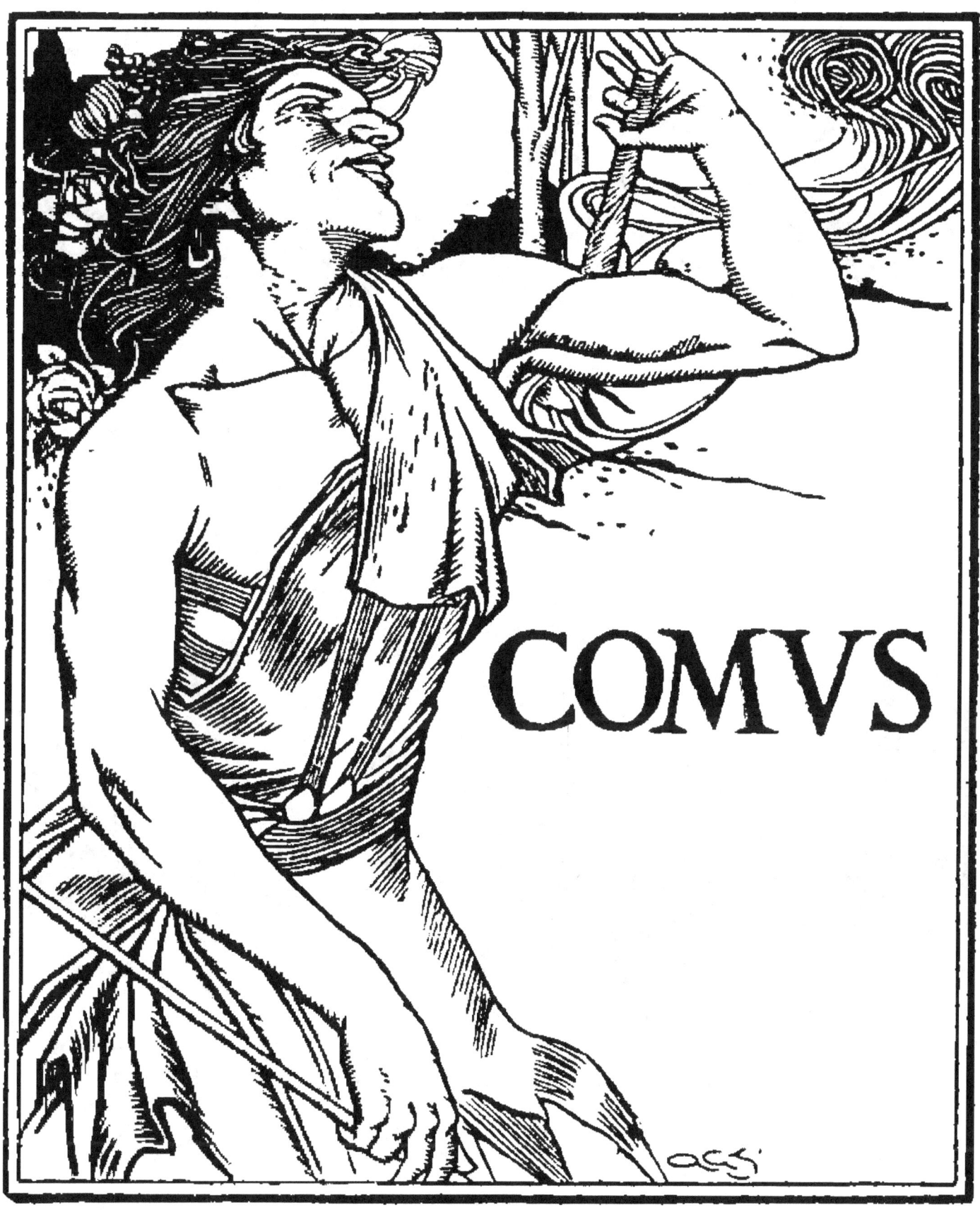

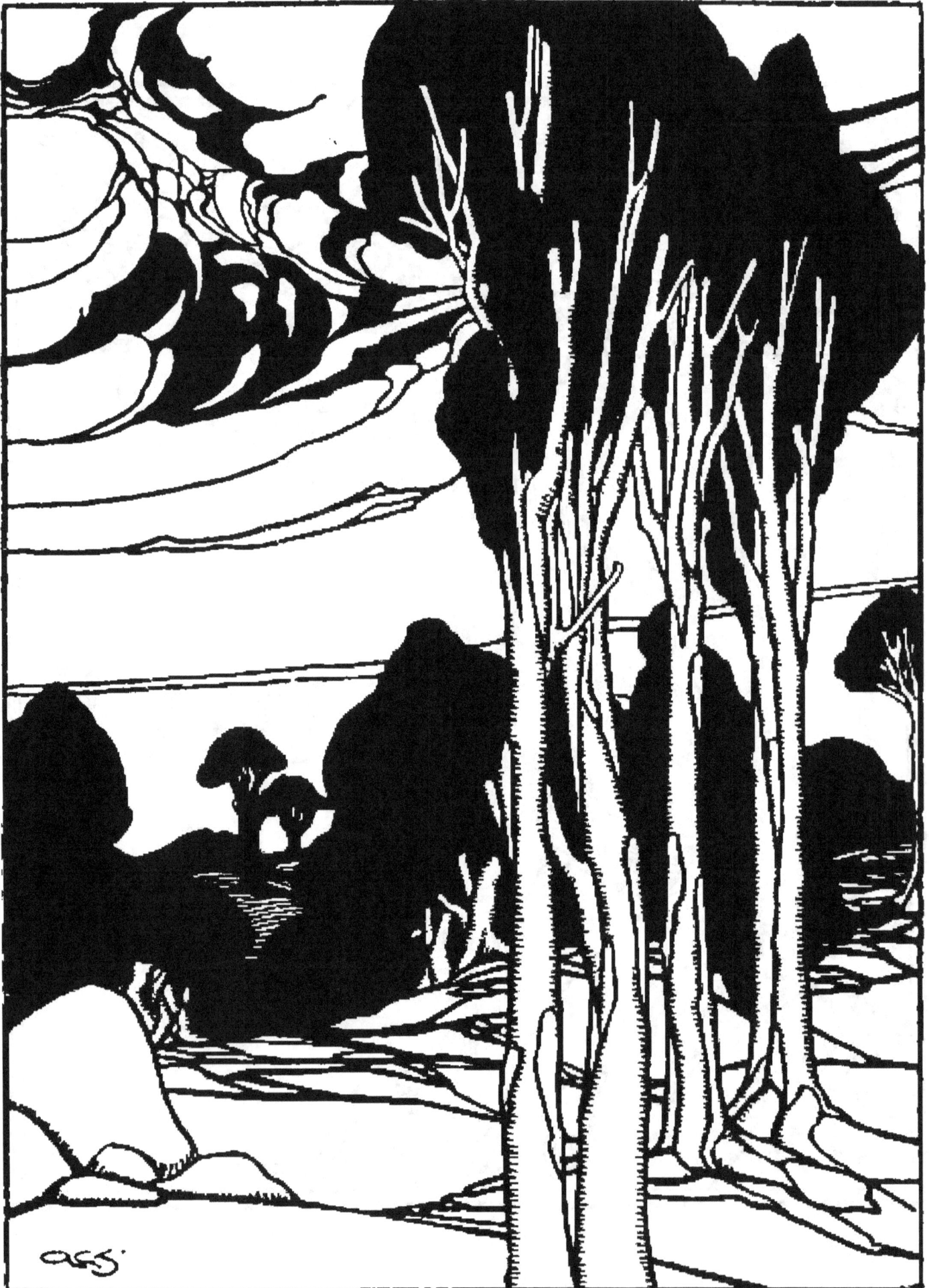

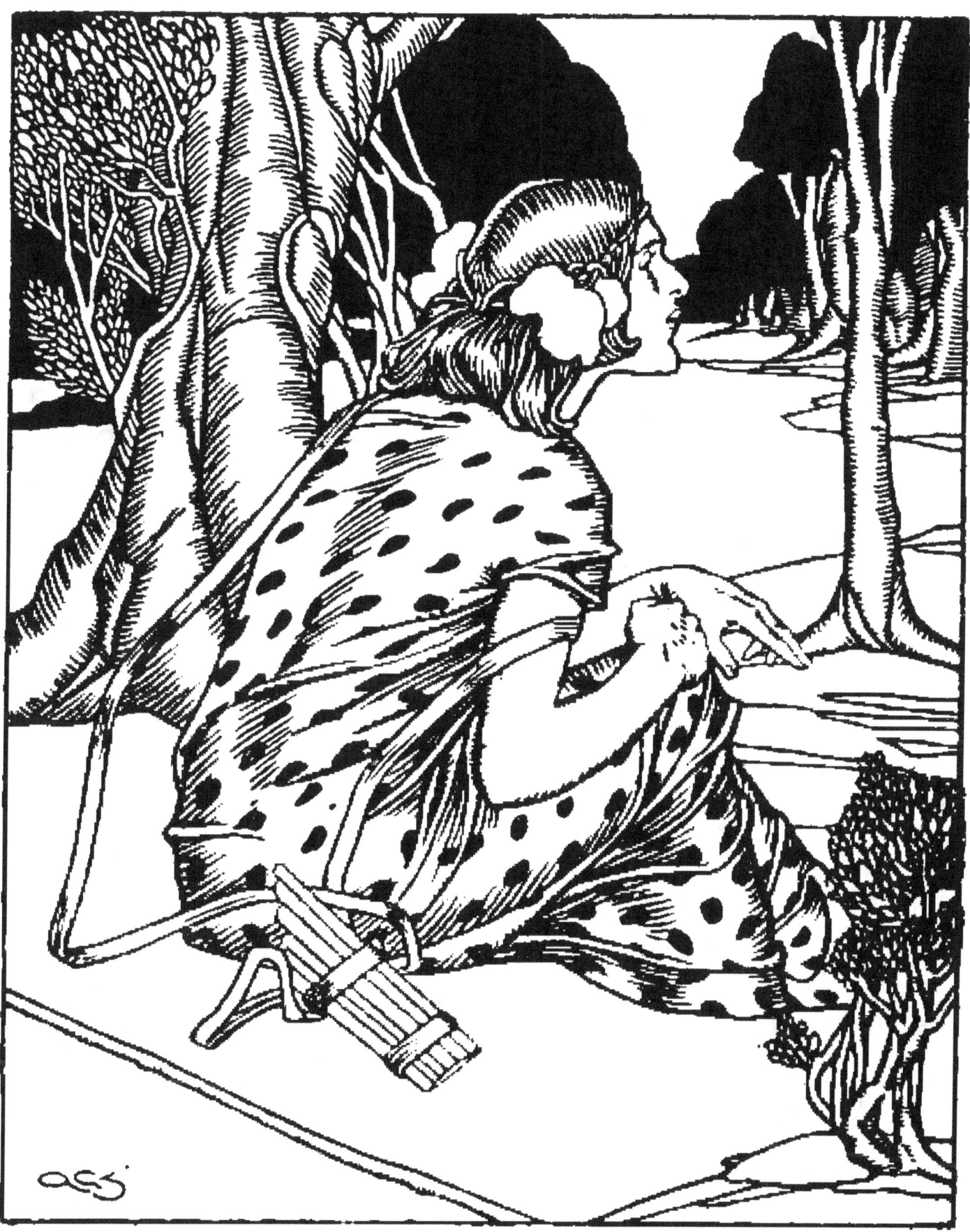

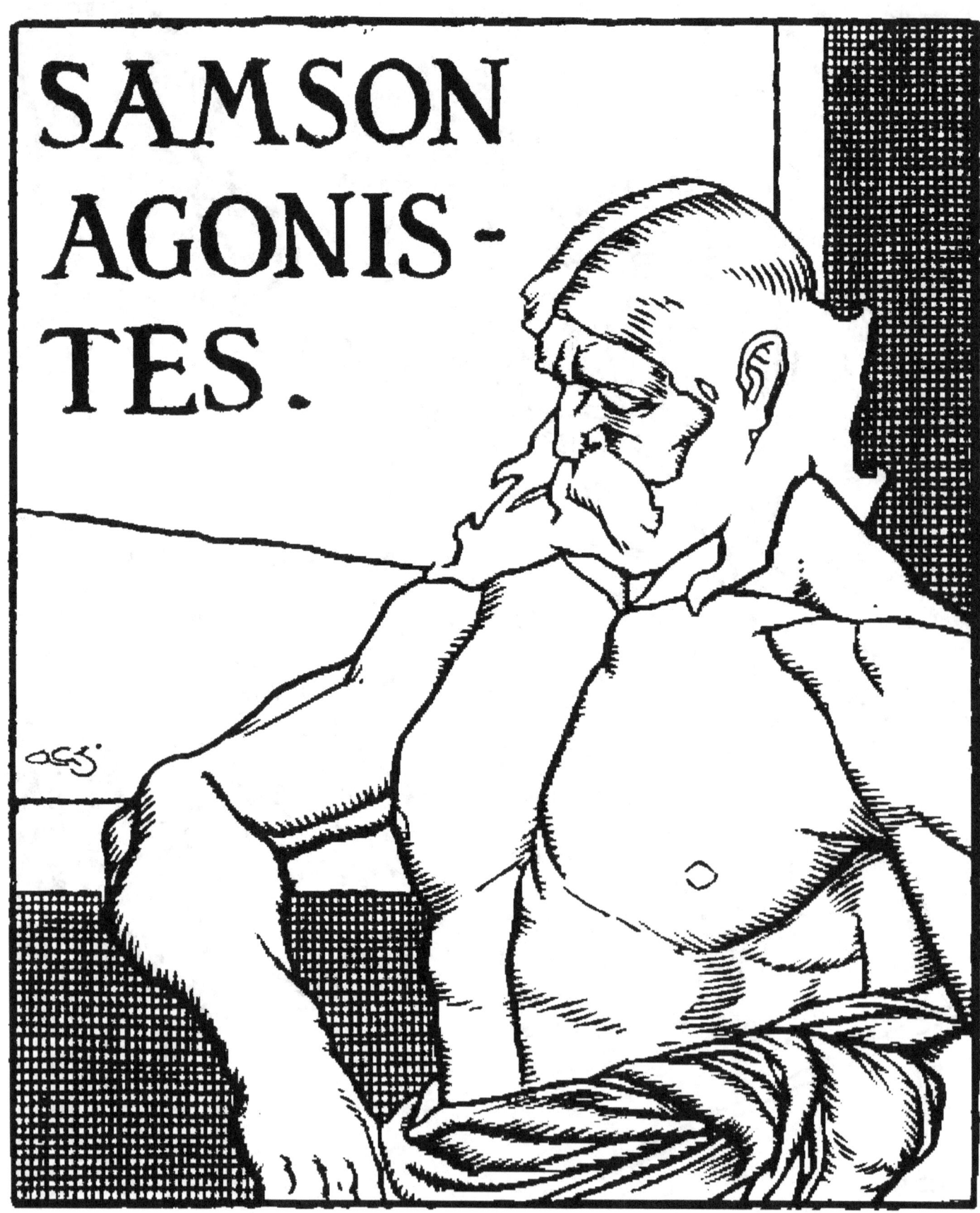

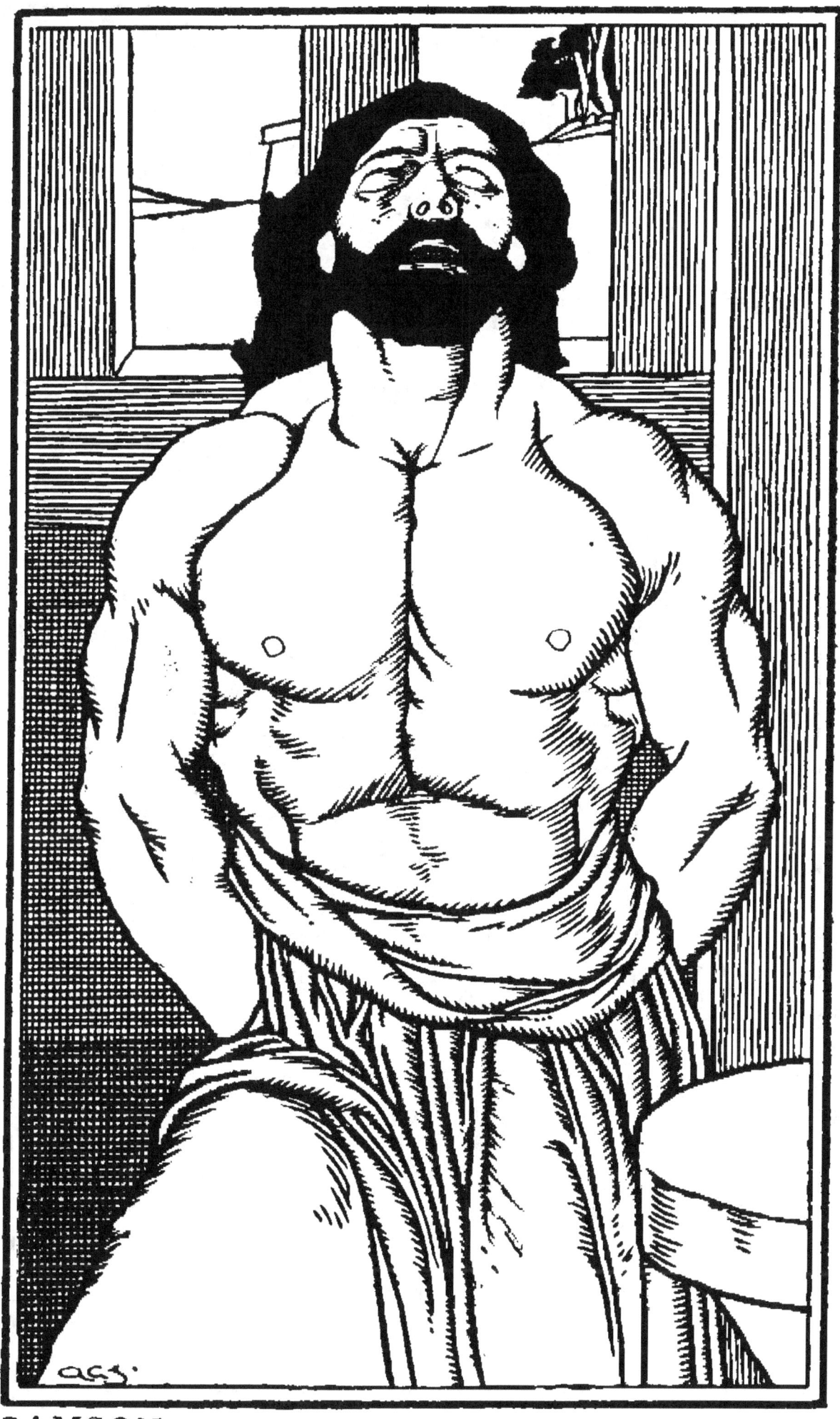

SAMSON

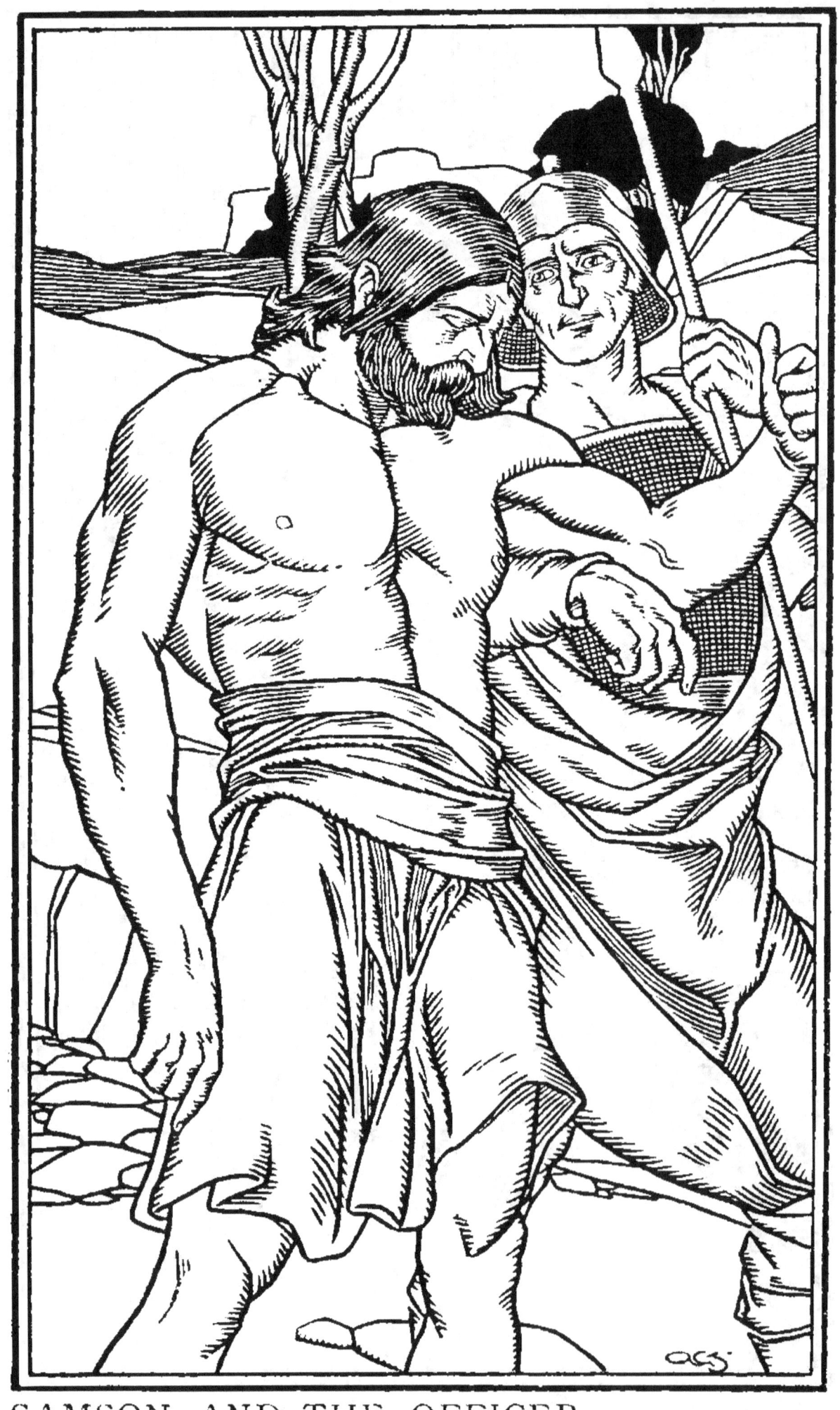

SAMSON AND THE OFFICER

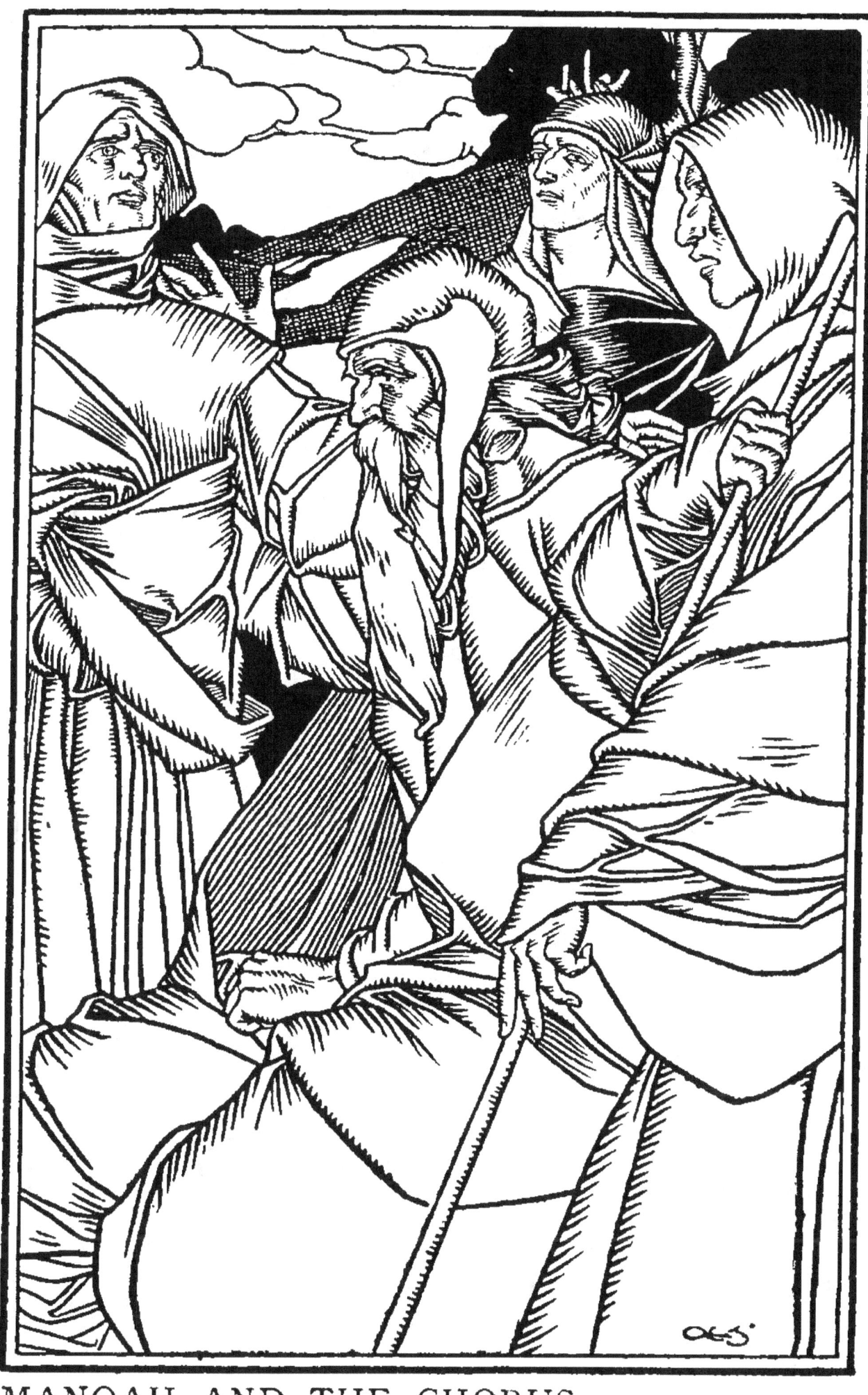

MANOAH AND THE CHORUS

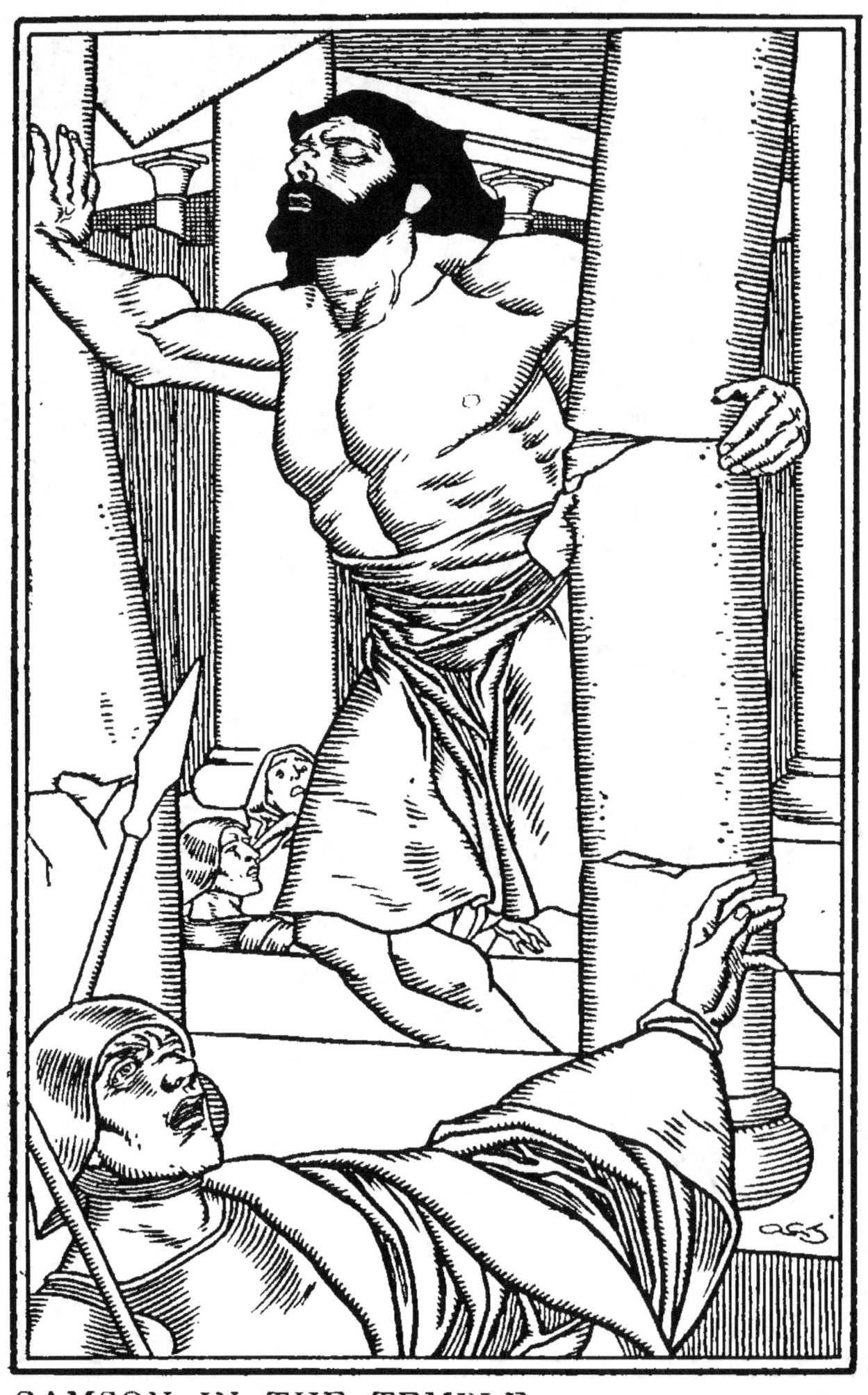

SAMSON IN THE TEMPLE

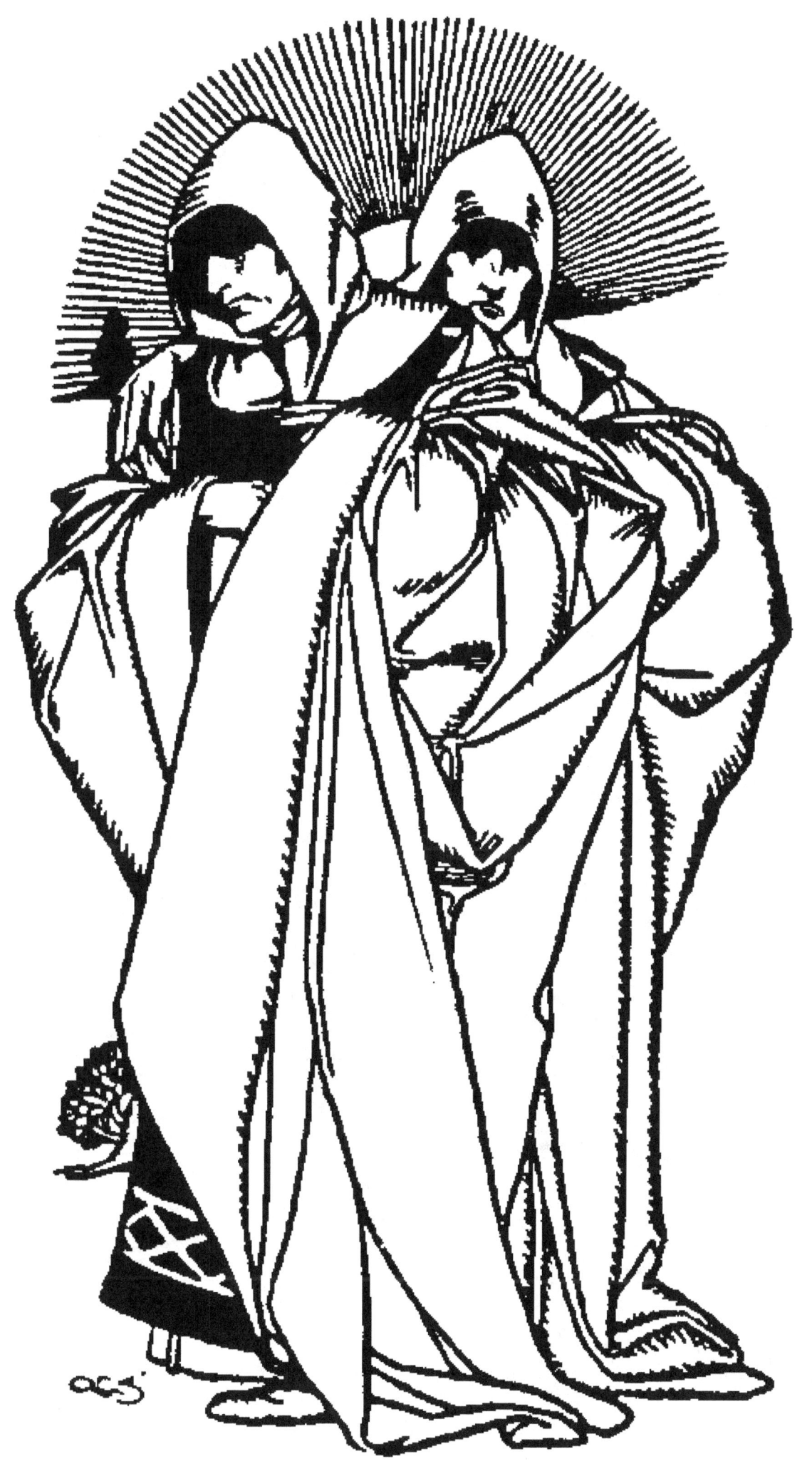

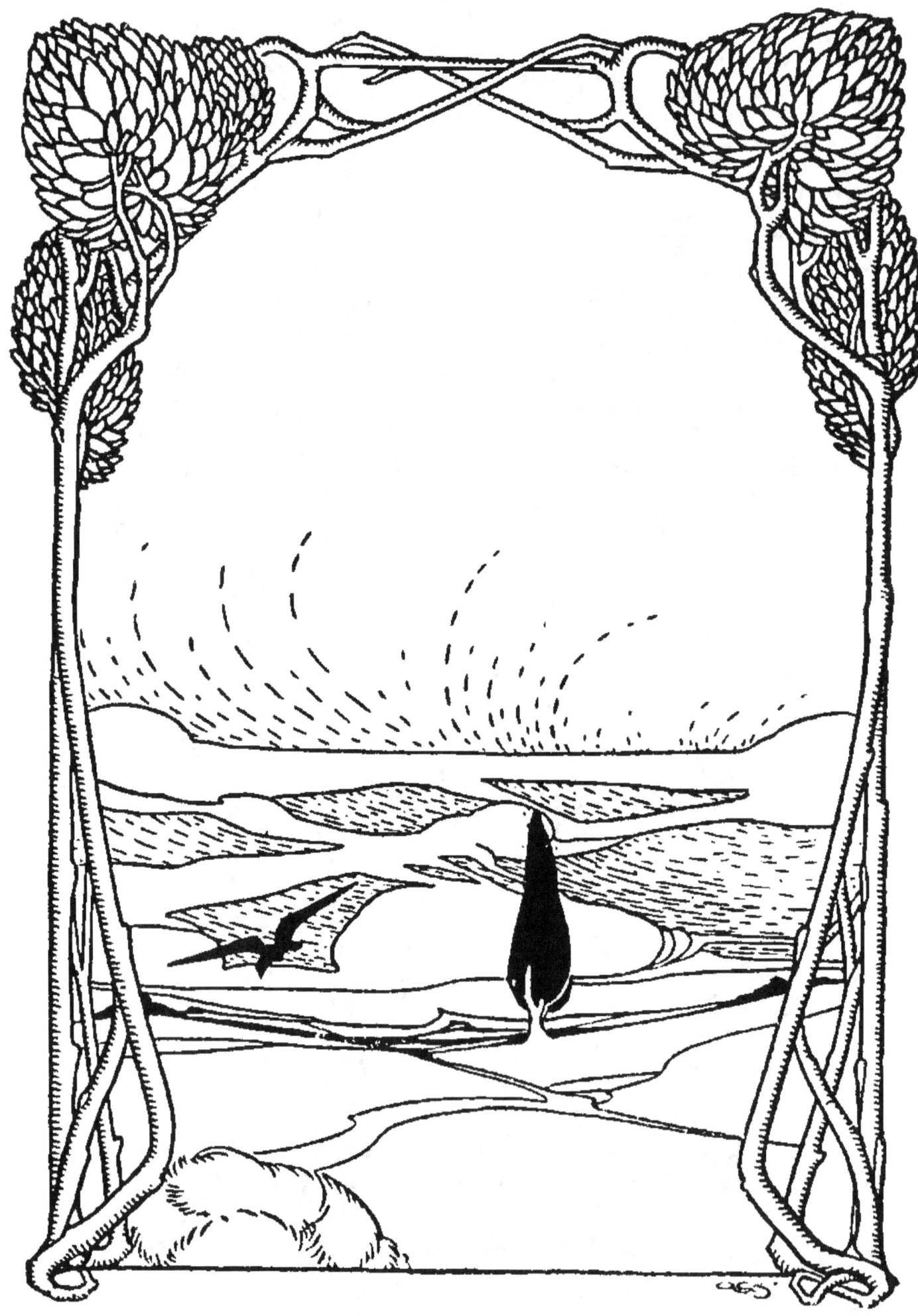

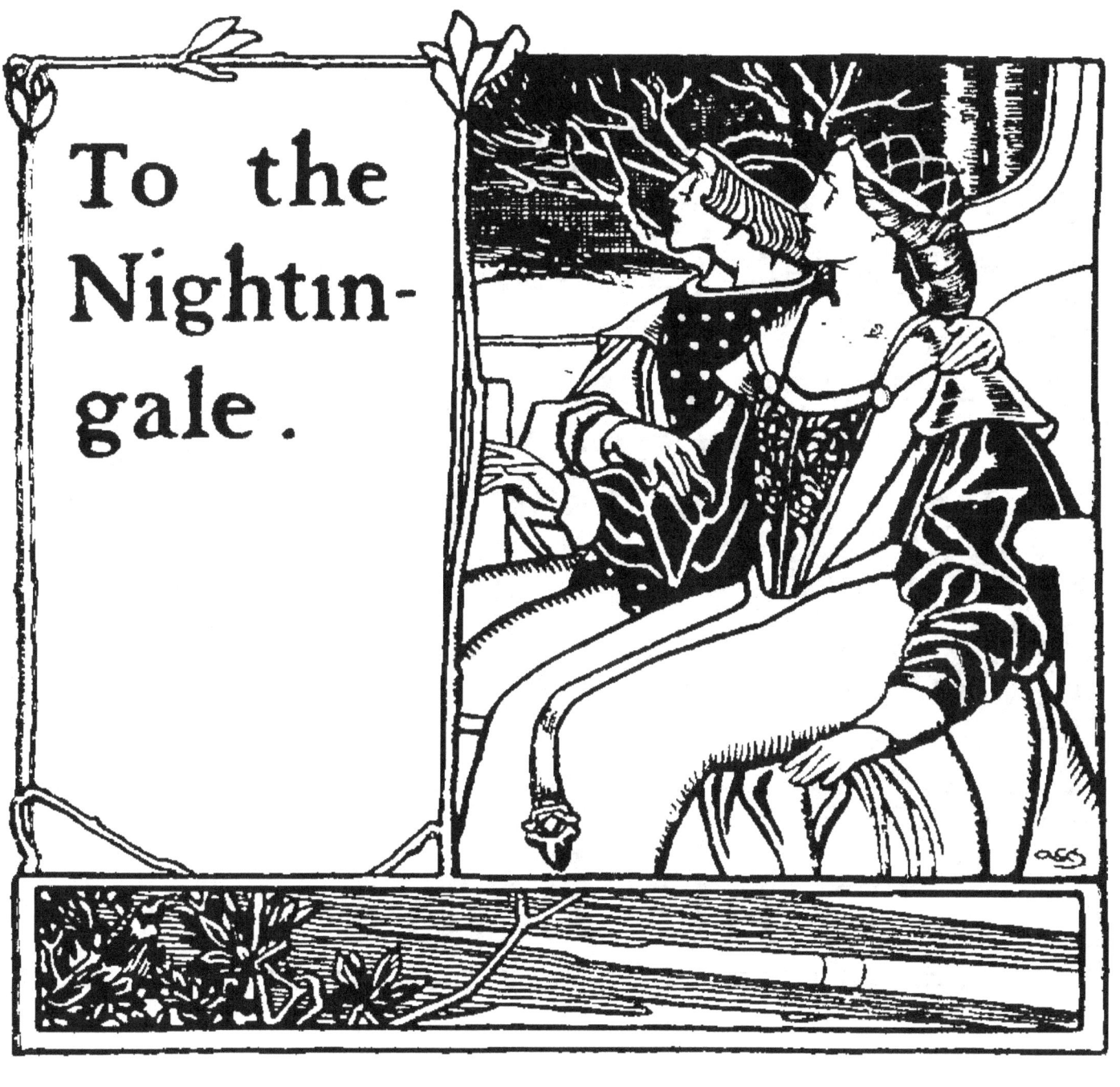

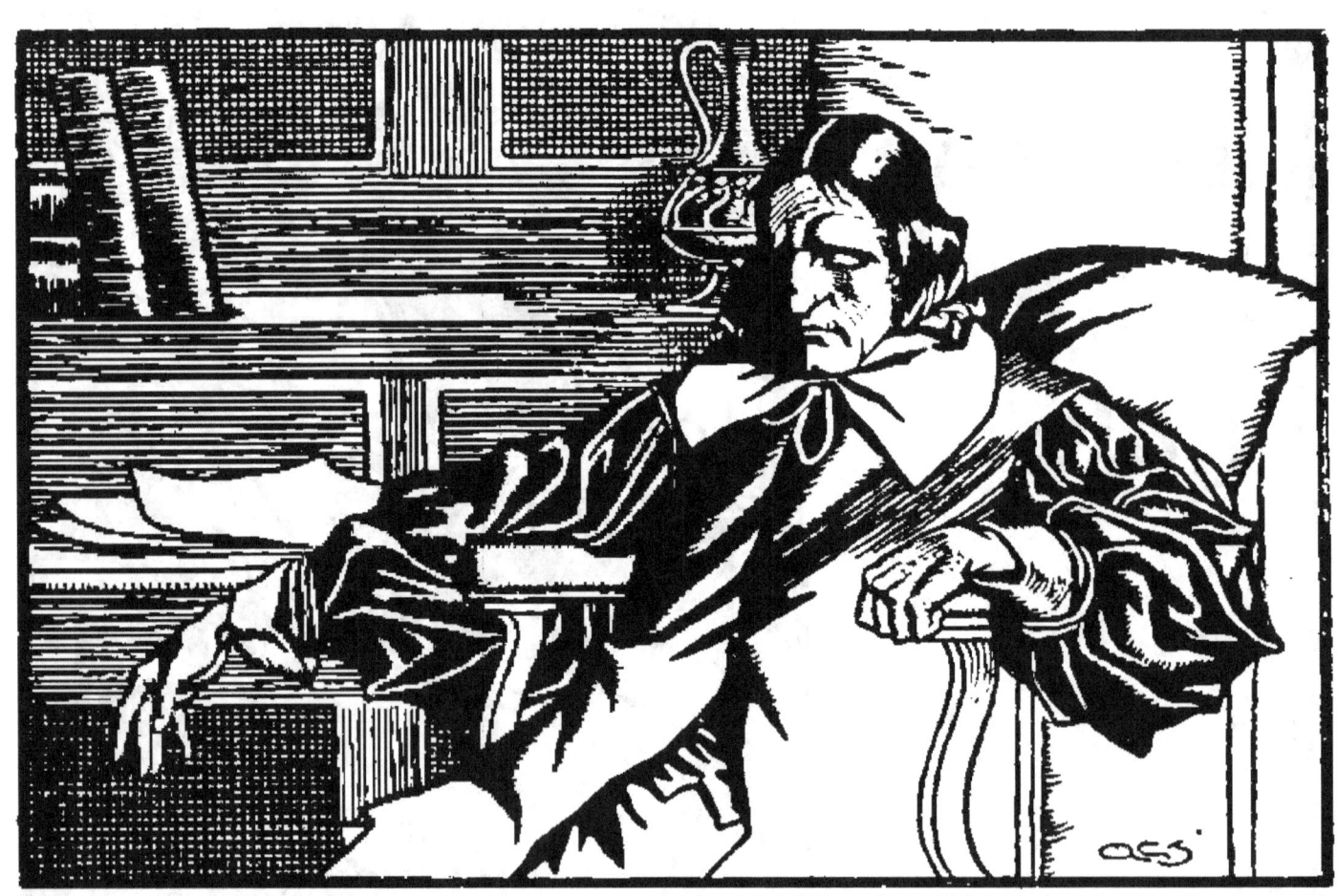

On his Blindness.

www.ingramcontent.com/pod-product-compliance
Lightning Source LLC
Chambersburg PA
CBHW082258220526
45469CB00009B/3052